DURBAN 1942:

A BRITISH TROOPSHIP REVOLT

DURBAN 1942:
A BRITISH TROOPSHIP REVOLT

GERRY R. RUBIN

THE HAMBLEDON PRESS
LONDON   AND   RIO GRANDE

Published by The Hambledon Press, 1992
102 Gloucester Avenue, London NW1 8HX (U.K.)
P.O. Box 162, Rio Grande, Ohio 45672 (U.S.A.)

ISBN 1 85285 080 9

© Gerry R. Rubin 1992

A description of this book is available from
the British Library and from the Library of Congress

Printed on acid-free paper and bound in
Great Britain by Cambridge University Press.

Contents

Introduction		vii
Acknowledgements		ix
1	The City of Canterbury	1
2	Prelude to Mutiny	19
3	Mutiny or Protest?	37
4	The Servicemen's Story	55
5	Records, Recriminations and Reform	79
6	The South African Connection	91
7	Like Other Mutinies?	105
8	Conclusions	123
Notes		129
Index		143

Introduction

On December 7 1941 Japanese military forces launched attacks on Pearl Harbor, Hong Kong, Malaya and the Philippines. Singapore was under threat, and after that, who could say whether Australia was still safe from invasion? The British service chiefs, having sent reinforcements to Burma and to India in the expectation of Japanese attacks against those countries, were now feverishly redirecting troops and weapons to Singapore and the Dutch East Indies. The South African port of Durban was a crucial transit point in this traffic. One convoy had arrived from the UK *en route* to Suez and a large number of troops were to change ships on January 12 1942. Among them were Royal Air Force ground crew whose new home for the three-week voyage to Singapore was to be the 8,000 ton troopship, *City of Canterbury*.

As the ship was not due to depart until the afternoon of January 13, all servicemen had been allowed shore leave on the 12th till midnight. However, by the early hours of the morning of the 13th, about 300 to 400 men had not returned on board. As an official report recorded,

> ... there was a certain amount of riotous behaviour amongst them in the dock area, due to complaints regarding the state of the ship, i.e. dirty, bug-infested, lousy, lack of lifebelts etc. By 0400 hours on the 13th these men had returned to the ship and apparently spent the night on board. On the following morning, the general behaviour of the men had taken a more serious turn, and although sentries appear to have been placed on the gangways, the men left the ship as and when they pleased. By 1100 hours, there were some 300–400 on the dockside indicating that they did not intend to sail on the *City of Canterbury*.

Officers appeared on the scene and addressed the men. A shot was fired from an officer's revolver, persuading some servicemen to board the ship. But nearly 200 maintained their refusal. The ship then set sail, just fifteen minutes behind schedule, leaving these men behind on the quayside. They were later marched off to a transit camp and preparations were made to try them for mutiny.

This book explores that episode on the quayside at Durban, both through official eyes and through the words and feelings of the servicemen themselves, a number of whom, fifty years later, recalled the events. It also examines what happened to some of the servicemen after the court-martial hearings and analyses the sensitive political context of South Africa in wartime where the incident occurred. Thus we will see how the courts martial generated local controversy and how they related to wider political pressures prevalent in the Union at the time. The unrest on board the *City of Canterbury* is also placed alongside other well-known or less well-known servicemen's protests and mutinies of the time, though no claim is made that the Durban incident was unique or of major importance in the history of the British armed forces.

What became of the servicemen who remained aboard the *City of Canterbury* for her voyage to the Far East will also be briefly discussed. In sharp contrast to those left behind at Durban, the vast majority of those proceeding to Singapore (and thence to the Dutch East Indies) became immediately caught up in the Allied collapse in the Far East. For the military personnel and some of the airmen who disembarked from the *City of Canterbury* at Singapore, there remained just ten more days of freedom before Singapore surrendered. For those airmen who were kept on board until the ship docked at Tandjong Priok, the port of Batavia (now Djakarta) in Java, there remained a month's respite, after which they endured three-and-a-half years of captivity in Japanese prison camps where survival from one day to the next was an unremitting struggle from which many did not return.

The story recounted is worth telling, not because it deflates overpomposity among the officer class (there is not much evidence in our study of this vice, though it probably existed in some quarters during the war). It is worth narrating because it tells us about life aboard a wartime troopship and it also tells us about an "Other Ranks" war, non-combatants at that, both those who experienced the formalised procedures of Air Force and Military Law and those whose war in the Far East was all too brief and melancholy.

Acknowledgements

Perhaps more than any other work which I have published, this book could not have been written without the cooperation of many individuals to whom I remain indebted. It was they who willingly shared with me their memories of the troopship, *City of Canterbury*, during World War II, and whose stories I have sought to incorporate in this history. Their names are too numerous to mention here, but particular thanks are due to Bernard Finch, Norwich; J.C. Smith, Cardiff; and Les Stubbs, Bromsgrove.

For kindly consenting to be interviewed, I would also like to thank Ron Carter, Sheffield; William Docherty, Glasgow; Joe Fishwick, Peterlee, Co. Durham; Christopher Goodall, Maidstone; William Kinnear, Glasgow; David Peacock, Ashford, Kent; the late Robert Peaty, Winchester; David Sharp, Greenock; Alex Smith, Paisley; and James Thomson, Glasgow.

Once again, the secretarial office at Darwin College, University of Kent, has performed superbly in producing a typescript with immense speed and efficiency. To Mabel Field, Ann Hadaway and Jenny Schunmann, my sincere gratitude. Sue Macdonald's vitality and warmth will, however, be sorely missed and the office will be a sadder place as a result.

For wholly different reasons, I also wish to thank those many persons who helped me through a difficult period when this work was being completed. Though this is by no means an exhaustive list, I would like to mention in particular Paddy Ireland and Joanne Conaghan, Alan Thomson, Barry Hooker, Derek Whittaker, Freda Vincent, Katherine O'Donovan, Pauline Scola, Richard de Friend, Séan Glynn, Stewart Miller, and Peter Brown, the Master of Darwin College at the University of Kent at Canterbury. Above all, I will be forever indebted to my wonderful Brenda, my sister and brother-in-law, Maxine and Stanley, and the most generous and supportive Heather Hooper and John Wightman.

Finally, I must acknowledge the generosity of the British Academy and the Nuffield Foundation in awarding me grants to cover research expenses.

G.R.R.

The City of Canterbury
November 1991

To my sons, Ilan and Gareth, with love

Chapter 1

The City of Canterbury

The *City of Canterbury*, according to those who sailed on her, was a lucky ship. It is somewhat ironic, therefore, that her condition, while in dock at Durban in January 1942, should provoke 200 servicemen to *refuse* to sail on her. In one respect, the luckier ones were indeed those who stayed behind on the quayside. For the fate awaiting most of those who remained on board and who put up with the uncomfortable conditions was, eventually, to be imprisonment or worse at the hands of the Japanese; three-and-a-half years of incarceration for those who managed to survive. The "mutineers" (for taking part in a mutiny was in fact with what they were originally charged) seem by contrast to have had a less stressful wartime experience after the Durban incident. Servicing trainers and other planes, in an India mercifully free from Japanese invasion, was the task most of them fulfilled after the Durban courts-martial. The *City of Canterbury* may indeed have been a lucky ship in avoiding bombs and shells at Suda Bay in Crete, Singapore Harbour and the Normandy beaches. The luck, for those who stayed on board at Durban, was double-edged.

The *City of Canterbury* was built in 1923 by Swan Hunter & Wigham Richardson of Newcastle for the City Line Ltd., a company with registered offices at 75 Bothwell Street, Glasgow.[1] The City Line, in turn, was part of the Ellerman group of companies. The *City of Canterbury* joined a fleet of other "City" ships, whose most famous, because most tragic, sister was probably the *City of Benares*, sunk by a U-boat in mid-Atlantic with the loss of over 90 evacuee children in September 1940.[2] As we shall see, a further link between the *City of Canterbury* and the *City of Benares* was that R.W.J. Hetherington served as First Officer on both ships.

The *City of Canterbury* with which we are concerned was not the first ship to honour the name of the premier cathedral city of England. According to the *Mercantile Navy List*, an early steam vessel bearing

Durban 1942: A British Troopship Revolt

the name *City of Canterbury* had been built some time before 1857. She was 154 tons and 120 h.p. and registered in London. The published history of the Ellerman Line, James Taylor's *Ellerman's: A Wealth of Shipping*,[3] mentions another *City of Canterbury*, built in 1875 by Barclay Curle shipyard in Glasgow. A steamer of 3,416 tons, she came to grief in 1897 when she was wrecked on the notorious James and Mary Shoal in the Hooghly River in India. A photograph of that unfortunate tea-carrying vessel appears in Taylor's book.[4]

The twentieth-century *City of Canterbury* with which we are concerned was a single-screw passenger and cargo liner of 8,549 tons, and deadweight capacity of 10,200 tons.[5] In peacetime, she provided accommodation for 130 first-class and 48 second-class passengers, though was certificated for 212 passengers. Her pre-war crew certification was for 148. She was $148' \times 56' \times 31'$ in dimension and was driven by a quadruple-expansion engine built at Wallsend, giving 4,250 h.p. Her boilers were coal burning (though converted to oil late on in her career), and her speed was around 12–13 knots. According to Bowen in his article in *Sea Breezes*, the ship was of a type favoured by the Ellerman Group in the pre- and post-First World War period. Thus she was a liner of moderate size and speed which was both an "admirable dividend-earner" and popular with travellers who preferred moderate rather than luxurious comfort.

In the early years, she served on the City Line's India routes, though was sometimes diverted to East African or South African ports. In 1930 her engine was given an exhaust turbo-electric drive, in place of the turbine being connected directly to the shaft, the aim being to improve her efficiency. This was apparently appreciated by Indian Army officers returning from home leave, if the vessel should otherwise be delayed by causes such as bad weather.

In the period from her launching till her requisitioning by the government in May 1940, she had completed 53 voyages. For example, voyage number 33, commencing on December 14 1933, saw her leave Hull on the 16th. She then proceeded to Antwerp, Rotterdam, Hamburg, London, Madeira, Cape Town, Mossel Bay, Algoa Bay, East London, Lourenço Marques, then back to Durban and the reverse journey, more or less, to Hull, arriving there on March 8 1934. Perhaps more typical of her pre-war voyages was number 41. This left Glasgow on March 23 1936 and proceeded to Liverpool,

The City of Canterbury

Gibraltar, Marseilles, Port Said, Suez, Perim, Bombay, Karachi and back to Glasgow on July 2, via most of the ports visited on the outward voyage. In the early months of the war, while still in owner service, she continued to sail the Middle East, Indian Ocean and South Africa route. From May to November 1940 she was assigned to the Liner Division of the Ministry of War Transport, then from November 1940 onwards she became His Majesty's Troopship *City of Canterbury*, certificated to carry 1,371 troops, including 101 in cabin accommodation.

Her first significant wartime role was as commodore ship of the Glasgow section of Convoy WS 5A which arrived in South Africa on January 26 1941, having left the Clyde on Christmas Day 1940. Details of the convoy are available from a number of sources, not least in the *SAWAS Book of Thanks*, a commemorative volume published in 1980 and dedicated to the South African Women's Auxiliary Services which provided hospitality for crewmen and servicemen arriving at South African ports during the war. The SAWAS Book lists all the WS convoy ships which arrived in South Africa and contains the names of many servicemen transported on those ships.

As Behrens notes in her history of merchant shipping during the war:

> Before the fall of France the only troops that had moved overseas in large numbers had been moved across the Channel, a voyage that can be performed in a matter of hours and in ships that could not be sent to the Indian Ocean area . . . and most of the passenger-cargo liners, that later formed the mainstay of the trooping fleet, were used exclusively for carrying cargo. This state of affairs, however, came abruptly to an end when the Mediterranean was closed, when the war started in the Middle East, and when the battle areas were no longer 200 miles across the sea, but 13,000.[6]

Once Churchill had made the decision to reinforce Egypt against attack from the Axis powers, trooping convoys were formed, and between August and December 1940, 77,000 troops were sent from the United Kingdom to the Middle East via the Cape. The WS convoys, codenamed thus after the initials of the Prime Minister, but nicknamed "Winston Specials", commenced in June 1940, making the long haul across the South Atlantic, via Africa to the Red Sea. Later, to counter Japanese intentions, convoys also transported troops and equipment to India and the Far East. As we shall see in later chapters, the Durban mutiny occurred when servicemen, who had been sent out from the United Kingdom in WS 14 in large passenger liners destined for the Middle East, refused to sail on the *City of Canterbury*, to which they had been transferred at Durban in order to proceed to Singapore (though the actual destination was the subject only of rumour initially).

In 1941 the average monthly number of troops carried on WS convoys was 29,000; for the last five months of 1941 it was 36,000. From the beginning of 1942, the Chiefs of Staff identified the following major challenges: (a) the stabilisation of the Far East; (b) the security of the Middle East; and (c) the security of India and the Indian Ocean bases. To achieve these aims, the Chiefs of Staff estimated that the monthly rate of troop movements must rise to 70,000. The shortage of sufficient numbers of troopships meant that this aim would prove impossible to attain, if other defensive war aims, for example, in the Western Desert, were to be met.[7]

Expedients to tackle the problem were devised. Load-carrying capacity on ships was increased. More efficient use of vessels was made, so that ships carrying troops outwards on WS routes, might, for example, return via North America, carrying troops thence to the UK. In particular, more meticulous planning of convoys was undertaken by the Ministry of War Transport from August 1941. For it was recognised that complications arose from the earliest stage of a convoy's life:

> To decide what personnel should be embarked when there was never enough room for all it was desired to dispatch; to organise their movement to the ports and their embarkation; and finally to get the convoy and its escorts out to sea, involved the co-operation of a multitude of authorities and committees ranging from the Chiefs of Staff downwards; and even when at last the convoy sailed . . . a hundred hazards lay ahead and much of the planning still remained to be translated into action.[8]

It had to reach its destination via a number of ports which had to be in readiness for its arrival; the planning of the homeward-bound voyages (usually by single ships without escorts) had likewise to be undertaken; and finally, it had to be timetabled such that the ships in convoy WS 7, for example, should be available for subsequent duty with, say, convoy WS 12.

The City of Canterbury

Organisational improvements were reflected in the categorisation of troopships for use on particular routes. The WS class were mainly passenger liners of between 17,000 and 18,000 tons on average, with speeds of 15 knots or more. Those who sailed on convoy WS 5A with the *City of Canterbury* will be mentioned shortly. But it is interesting to note that on completion of that voyage, the *City of Canterbury* was retained on service in the Indian Ocean region. Ships ploughing this route were in fact a second category of troopships, considered unsuitable for the Atlantic routes. For, at a speed of less than 15 knots, they could not outrun German submarines. The final category was the "Monsters", that is, the *Queen Elizabeth*, *Queen Mary*, *Mauretania*, *Aquitania*, *Ile de France* and the *Nieuw Amsterdam*. All were more than 35,000 tons gross and, with speeds considerably in excess of 20 knots, they could easily outrun enemy submarines.[9] With this tripartite structure, it was laid down that no WS ships, with troops destined for the Middle East, should proceed beyond Durban. Instead, the servicemen would be transhipped at Durban for onward passage to Suez or India in ships deemed unsuitable for the Atlantic routes. With the outbreak of war against Japan, onward passage to the Far East would become an additional itinerary. As we shall see, the voyage of the Durban "mutineers" was intended to comply with this arrangement.

The operation of the WS convoy system did in fact improve considerably after reorganisation. Whereas the average number of troops shifted in WS convoys between August and December 1941 had been 36,000, the figure for February to May 1942 was over 65,000.[10] At the same time, troop-carrying provision on other routes had also improved, most relevantly in the case of the *City of Canterbury* between India and the Far East; and India and Australia and the Middle East. The *City of Canterbury* herself was to spend much of the second half of 1941 in shuttling troops between Suez or Alexandria and Durban in CM convoys. But this was all in the future, months after the completion of convoy WS 5A.

That convoy signalled the departure of the *City of Canterbury* from United Kingdom waters until her return in May 1944, in preparation for the D-Day landings. WS 5A was a large convoy of 12 cargo and 20 troopships carrying 30,000 troops, unaware that they were destined for the Middle East. In the days prior to her departure the crew, who were mainly Glaswegians and Lascars, the latter with their distinctive blue dungaree uniforms, busied themselves, under the watchful eye of Regimental Quartermaster-Sergeant Dobinett, with preparing the ship for the embarkation of the troops. The bulk of servicemen were from the 89th Heavy Anti-Aircraft (HAA) Regiment, Royal Artillery, who were to remain with Middle East Forces till 1943, when they were transferred to the Italian campaign.[11] According to the diary of events kept by the troop deck sergeant-major on the *City of Canterbury*, Mr T. McGill of Edinburgh (ex-Royal Armoured Corps), on Monday, December 16 1940 he and his fellow crew members had been issuing hammocks and blankets to the troops all day and did not finish till late at night. The following afternoon the ship left the King George V Dock in Glasgow and sailed down the Clyde with 1,480 troops on board,[12] in excess of the numbers stipulated in the Ministry of War Transport papers.[13] While passing the shipyards of the Clyde, McGill recorded that, "all the workmen in the shipbuilding yards cheered us and people standing on the banks waved handkerchiefs, and other ships started blowing their sirens. I am beginning to feel downhearted as I know that very soon we will be far away from our homeland".[14] She anchored at the Tail of the Bank (Gourock) the same evening, and on the following day anti-aircraft guns were fixed and manned, degaussing tests were made and compasses adjusted. In the afternoon her master, Captain Herbert Percival, attended a convoy conference together with Captain May RN, the Naval Control Officer, Captain Radcliffe RNR, Assistant Naval Control Officer, a vice-admiral (possibly Sir Roderick Macdonald), the captains of the aircraft carriers *Furious* and *Argus*, the captain of the anti-aircraft cruiser *Bonaventure*, and captains of other warships, mostly destroyers. Also attending, of course, were the masters of the other troopships in the Glasgow portion of the convoy. These ships were the *Neuralia*, *Ernebank*, *Costa Rica*, *Mahseer*, *Barrister*, *Adviser*, *Arabistan*, *Leopoldville*, *Benvinnes* and *Empire Trooper*. The last-named had been a pre-war German "Strength Through Joy" vessel which the Hitler regime had provided for holiday cruises for workers.[15] She had subsequently been captured from the Germans and, together with *Arabistan*, was to suffer damage in an engagement during the convoy. Some of the ships were, as their names suggested, Belgian, Free French or Dutch.

The City of Canterbury

The Glasgow convoy set sail from Gourock at 2100 hours on December 18 1940, and joined the Liverpool portion of WS 5A in the North Channel the following morning. In the Liverpool section were the merchant ship *Tamaroa*, with Rear-Admiral Raine as commodore, *Orbita* as vice-commodore, and *Settler*, *City of London*, *City of Derby*, *Bhutan*, *Rangitiki*, *Menelaus*, *Elisabethville*, *Anselm*, *Delane* and *Stentor*. In addition to the naval vessels listed previously, some sloops and corvettes escorted the convoy at different intervals. The destroyers included Royal Navy manned lend-lease vessels from the United States, with their distinctive four funnels.

After the two portions of the convoy converged, progress was uneventful until 3 a.m. on Friday, December 20 when dense fog suddenly developed and *Menelaus* and *City of London* collided. On the night of December 21–22 all the destroyers and sloops parted company, leaving the convoy with four corvettes and *Bonaventure*. Overhead, planes were keeping a lookout for enemy submarines, a threat which meant that the troops aboard the ships were ordered to sleep in full dress. The convoy itself was formed six abreast, with five or six ships in each column. All the troopships were in the centre of the convoy, with the merchantmen on the outside. On the morning of December 23, the convoy was joined by the merchant ships *Northern Prince*, *Essex*, *Empire Song*, *Clan Morrison* and *Clan Cummings*, by the aircraft carriers *Furious* and *Argus* (which replaced another carrier, *Formidable*, which had departed the previous day) and by another anti-aircraft cruiser. Later that day an air attack was expected but did not materialise, and finally the cruisers *Berwick* and *Dunedin* joined the convoy. The aircraft carriers were heavily laden on open deck with crated fighter aircraft bound for Takoradi, on the Gold Coast, West Africa. The aircraft would be assembled there and then flown across central Africa and up to Egypt.

On board the *City of Canterbury* herself, the crew and passengers had to contend initially with sea-sickness, as the ship rolled about in rough weather. This rather lessened the problem which Captain Percival had identified at the outset. That was the shortage of mercantile cooks in Glasgow, forcing the regimental cooks to take over the cooking for the troops. Percival himself was critical of the cooking facilities aboard the ship, given the number of troops. He acknowledged that complaints were justifiable and agreed that some of the aft messes suffered. In addition, the heat in the troop kitchen was appalling during the nightly blackout. As the fore well deck was often awash in rough seas, the mess orderlies experienced great difficulty in carrying the food to the aft mess decks where 800 troops were billeted. No doubt, as the ship was being tossed about, the thoughts of many of the troops were on matters other than food.

Although the convoy started to zig-zag on December 22, Captain Percival on the following day relaxed the order to the troops to sleep in full dress, considering the ship to be outside the immediate danger area. He spoke too soon. At 5.45 a.m. on December 24, in the area of the Bay of Biscay, a heavy explosion was felt in the ship and flashes were seen off the starboard bow. It was dirty, south-eastern weather, with drizzle and a high wind. Percival thought that thunder might have caused the vibration but remained suspicious nonetheless. Off the Azores the next morning, Christmas Day, at 7.40 a.m. exactly the same kind of explosion was felt again. On this occasion there was no doubting the cause: the convoy was under shell attack from an enemy raider. Though rumour had it that she was the German pocket battleship, the *Scharnhorst*, she was in fact the 8-in. cruiser, *Admiral Hipper*. In the mist and drizzle Percival sighted the raider off the starboard bow for a brief few minutes. She was shelling the convoy, landing her shells slightly ahead of the *City of Canterbury*. Then she shifted close astern and hit the *Empire Trooper* with two shells and *Arabistan* with one. The convoy escorts fired back and HMS *Berwick*, a cruiser of similar size and power to the *Hipper* but of a much older design, chased the raider. During the brief encounter one of the escort destroyers went up and down the convoy, making a smokescreen to hide the convoy ships from the attacker. Eventually, after an exchange between the *Berwick* and the *Hipper*, during which each sustained some damage, the raider escaped in low visibility to Brest for repairs. The *Empire Trooper*, which herself had opened up on the *Hipper* with her own guns, was escorted to the Azores for repairs and then to Gibraltar, while *Arabistan* stayed with the convoy which had dispersed at 8.30 a.m. at full speed. Meanwhile HMS *Berwick* returned to the convoy, flashing a signal to the commodore ship that the raider was now distant from the convoy and that *Berwick* had managed to sink the *Hipper*'s supply ship, the *Borden*.

The City of Canterbury

In the confusion of the engagement the Dutch ship, *Costa Rica*, lost touch with the rest of the convoy and headed for Freetown, Sierra Leone, at full speed. However, after joining up with a cargo vessel, she was found by HMS *Shropshire* and escorted back to the convoy which had reassembled at noon on December 28. Christmas dinner on board the *City of Canterbury* was a joyous occasion after the news of the *Berwick*'s success. The following day it was found that two more aircraft carriers, *Illustrious* and *Atreus*, had joined the convoy. Spirits were high even though the *City of Canterbury* was sailing on her own until reassembly on the 28th.

After the encounter with the *Hipper*, the remainder of the voyage was uneventful. A Hogmanay party was held by the crew aboard the *City of Canterbury* with whisky supplied with the compliments of the ship's officers and with beer in good supply. On January 2 1941, tropical clothing was now being worn and the sea was calm. Three days later the convoy entered Freetown to replenish stores and to take on fresh water. No-one was allowed ashore but everyone was struck by the beauty of green palm trees and golden sand. Relieved of the gloom of a blackout, "All the ships looked like the Blackpool Illuminations; at night it was a lovely sight".[16] The pleasant atmosphere no doubt helped to dispel feelings of discomfort in the cramped conditions aboard ship, where the troops had to wash, shave as best they could, and bathe in sea water.

The convoy set sail again on January 8, briefly renewing acquaintance with the aircraft carrier *Formidable* on her maiden voyage. Soon it arrived at Durban on January 25, staying there for four days for bunkering and storing. Shore leave was permitted only during the afternoons, with each ship's contingent being assembled and marched through the streets of the city to a rousing welcome. Displays of Zulu dancing and musical entertainment by the legendary "Lady in White", Perla Gibson, kept the visitors occupied. On the 29th the convoy set off again and sailed in the direction of the Red Sea. Finally it arrived at Port Tewfik, Suez, on February 16, eight weeks and five days after leaving the United Kingdom. Percival reported that, on disembarkation, the troops were in "first class condition, and I have no hesitation in saying that it was a most successful voyage; the incident [sic] of sickness was practically Nil and the Troops left the ship looking smart, cheerful and well nourished".

Durban 1942: A British Troopship Revolt

From February 16 to March 7 1941 the *City of Canterbury* remained at anchor either in Suez Bay or below Newport Rock when the "Bay" became too congested. This was at a time when the Suez Canal was blocked by mines. Other ships in the convoy proceeded to other destinations. For example, the *City of Derby* off-loaded iron ore at Calcutta and loaded tea at Colombo before sailing homeward via Cape Town and Halifax, Nova Scotia.[17]

The situation in the Middle East was confused at the time and the *City of Canterbury* was given a number of different orders which were quite simply mistaken or changed at the last moment. Thus orders to take 1,000 Italian prisoners of war were issued and then rescinded in favour of instructions to transport 400 RAF personnel back to the UK. That instruction was, in turn, cancelled. The order to carry POWs was then reinstated, only to be set aside for a second time. Eventually orders were issued to proceed to Port Sudan, arriving on March 10 to join a convoy of five ships as far as Aden, leaving on March 12. The other four ships (all from WS 5A) were the *City of London* (commodore), the Dutch ship *Costa Rica*, the Belgian vessel *Elisabethville* and the ill-fated *Anselm*, later sunk by a U-boat in July 1941 with the loss of 254 RAF personnel. Off Aden, the *City of Canterbury* parted company and proceeded to Durban as a single unescorted ship, arriving there on March 26.

Her next role was to transport 1,500 troops in convoy to Suez. They were men of the 68th Heavy AA Regiment who had sailed out to Durban from the UK aboard a hurriedly converted refrigerator ship, the *Northumberland*. Their onward journey was to be one which anticipated some of the dissatisfaction with the *City of Canterbury* and which led to the "walk-off" at Durban the following January.

The embarkation of the 68th HAA for the Middle East where they soon formed part of the Eighth Army, commenced at 9 a.m. on March 30, and at 11.30 that morning, the troops were all on board. Percival paid tribute to the OC Troops, Colonel Llewellyn, for organising things so smoothly. One problem which was encountered, however, and which with hindsight probably affected discipline aboard the ship, was that it was difficult to obtain the necessary stores for the voyage, especially flour, ice, beer, biscuits and potatoes. Part of the difficulty was the presence at Durban of such a large convoy for such a short period of time. As we shall see, the organisation of shipping within South African ports during the war was a matter of some concern to the British authorities.

Eventually the convoy set off on Monday, March 31. There were at least 12 cargo and 18 troopships, and the escorts included HMS *Phoebe* and the cruisers HMS *Glasgow* and HMS *Cornwall*. The Royal Marines band aboard the last-named entertained the troops in the convoy as HMS *Cornwall* passed up and down the line of ships. The *Empress of Canada* passed the convoy as the liner made her way south. A number of breakdowns, however, dogged the progress of the convoy. On April 12 four ships stopped with engine trouble, forcing the convoy to slow down to enable them to catch up after repairs. On the 17th the main engine air pump on the *City of Canterbury* herself broke down, almost causing a collision with the *City of London*. Volunteers from among the troops on board who had engineering experience came forward and temporary repairs were effected. The volunteer engineers were rewarded with an invitation to dinner in the Officers' Saloon. Aboard the *City of Canterbury* troops and crew were kept informed of developments (subject to censorship, of course) through the daily issue of a news-sheet, the *Canterbury Tales*.[18] It was a mixture of snippets of world news, home news, shipboard news, anecdotes and jokes. The "official" daily paper (there may have been a rival, "unofficial" version), offered its readers the "Purser's Tale", the "Adjutant's Tale", the "OC Troops' Tale", and so on. The newsheet of April 19 1941 mixed leisure reportage with sadness. An item concerning a swimming competition held in the ship's pool was followed by a report of the death on board the ship of Gunner L.S. Brett, 200th HAA Bty, RA who died of pneumonia:

> This morning we said "Goodbye", in a simple ceremony, when we committed his earthly remains to the Deep. Our hearts were heavy at the thought of being so near the end of our journey, and not having our full complement. We extend our sympathy to Gnr. Brett's family and friends at Reigate. It will be a dark day for them when the news reaches home. It is surely symbolic that we should pay our last respects soon after sunrise; however dark the day for those left behind, it was sunrise for Gnr. Brett.

In his report to the owners, Captain Percival remarked that there had been slight dissatisfaction with the food during the voyage. The flour was not as good as it ought to have been and biscuits were occasionally issued in lieu of bread, "but on the whole", he concluded, "there should have been no complaints as the troops were well fed . . ." In fact, some of those who sailed on that voyage distinctly recall considerable discord on board the ship.

It has to be remembered that living conditions on the ship were extremely uncomfortable, indeed unpleasant, in warm climes. Sleeping accommodation for the troops was below deck in holds usually used for carrying cargo. All the floor space was covered by mattresses, and hammocks were slung across the hold. In this demanding, unventilated environment, to which the troops were unaccustomed, complaints about overcrowding, poor food and inadequate drinking water were quickly voiced. Leonard Dunn of Bradford, who was a corporal in the 276th HAA Bty (68th HAA Regt.), recalls that a number of "hotheads" among the troops created disruption which eventually led to the senior officers addressing the men and reading the "Riot Act" to the troops aboard the ship. During this dressing-down of the rank-and-file, some of the critical voices called out a few obscenities to the officers. As none of the ORs would "split" on who was responsible, the whole draft was put on extra and unnecessary routines. Dunn recalls that water was available for only one hour in the morning and one hour in the evening, and that each tap and washroom had a 24-hour guard put on them. In addition, all stairways to the open deck had a 24-hour guard and in effect all guard duties were doubled. Another veteran of 68th HAA Regt., J.L. Clarke of Derby (who was with the 200th HAA Bty.), was told that the rationing of the drinking water and the stationing of the guards was because the desalination plant had broken down, causing a severe shortage of water for the boilers. While he cannot confirm the incident of the senior officers reading the Riot Act to the troops, his vivid recollection of the uncomfortable conditions aboard the ship anticipates the trouble which was to erupt the following January in Durban. The biscuits which Captain Percival, in his report, mentioned were provided in substitution for bread, were themselves quite unpalatable. They were about 3" square, by ¼" thick and would be spread over the fo'c'sle by the Lascar crew, using stokers' shovels, in order to let them dry out and allow the weevils to trot out. The feeling among some at the time was that whereas the *Northumberland* had been quite uncomfortable, the smaller *City of Canterbury*, to which the men of the 68th HAA Regt. had been transferred at Durban, was significantly worse. As with the later incident in January 1942, the dissatisfaction may well have been increased by the forced removal of the troops from the hospitality of Durban, where a week's shore leave had been granted, to the deprivations on board a steamy, overcrowded vessel. None of the troops, needless to say, was expecting a luxury cruise to the Middle East, but for some the tolerance threshold had already been breached.

At length the *City of Canterbury* arrived in convoy at Suez on April 21, and the following day disembarked the troops at Port Said. This at least scotched one rumour going the rounds aboard the ship. That was that as a punishment for the trouble aboard the ship, the 68th HAA Regt. would be sent direct to Greece even though their AA guns were travelling with another convoy. However, by this time the evacuation of Greece had already started, so the 68th HAA were simply dumped at the dockside at Port Said for 24 hours, and then ordered to occupy trenches in the desert not very far from the ship. The rumour was, in fact, a close-run thing for, while discharging baggage and cargo on the quayside, the *City of Canterbury* took on board the charts necessary to navigate Greek waters. A number of other ships in the convoy carried on through the Suez Canal and into the Mediterranean, making for Crete where the defences were to be reinforced against the expected German invasion.

The *City of Canterbury* herself then spent the next few days sailing backwards and forward between Port Said and Alexandria, being given conflicting instructions at various intervals, even being told at one point that she was no longer needed for the government's Sea Transport Service. She remained at Port Said from April 28 to May 6 1941, during which time she embarked some 1,500 to 1,600 Royal Marines for a secret destination. This was later disclosed as Suda Bay in Crete from which Allied troops were to be hurriedly evacuated after the German paratroop invasion of the island on May 20.

The voyage to Suda Bay began inauspiciously as the air pump, which had given trouble on the previous convoy, broke down again. Assisted by volunteers among the marines, the ship's engineers got the air pump working again, and the *City of Canterbury* hurriedly rejoined her convoy, steaming at 12 knots in the company of the *Cape Horn*, the *Lossiebank* and the *Rawnsley* whose slow speed of 8 knots caused the convoy some delay. It was indeed a security-conscious convoy of one trooper, three supply vessels and six escorts, including the cruiser *Flamingo*.

The troops on board were the marines of the Mobile Naval Base Defence Organisation (MNBDO). According to John Hall Spencer in his account of the *Battle of Crete*,[19] the unit had been formed in 1935 in order to protect Alexandria against Mussolini's ambitions after Abyssinia. Its strength was 5,300 and in respect to Crete, the MNBDO was to be employed to augment the existing defences of the island, in order to ensure its survival as a fleet refuelling base. MNBDO's role was therefore considerably broadened in the light of the threat posed to the island after the German victory in Greece.

The first echelon which was aboard the *City of Canterbury* comprised mainly gunnery personnel. There were 62 officers under the command of Lt.-Colonel Sergeant, 88 senior NCOs and 1,171 corporals and marines. Further functional groupings included two three-inch AA batteries, two coast-defence batteries, the signal company, the boat company, half the landing company, half the transport company and a hospital designated "No. 1, Tented".[20]

On May 8 Captain Percival asked Col. Sergeant to take over the AA defence of the ship. The defences comprised a 4.7" for low flying aircraft, one Breder, ten Hotchkiss, one Holman, two strip Lewis and 24 Lewis, "all well manned and we hope to give a good account of ourselves if attacked". He did not have long to wait. After being spotted by Blenheim fighters which exchanged recognition signals with the Senior Officer Escort, the convoy was attacked by three or four enemy torpedo-bombers at 7.45 p.m.[21] The planes quickly departed, the Blenheims flew back and then disappeared again, then the attackers returned, appearing on the port quarter flying in line ahead. When abeam of the convoy, they turned towards the ships. Captain Percival saw an aircraft preparing a torpedo run, ordered "Hard to port", and instructed all the guns to open up. The aircraft attempted to pass over the ship, but in the face of the intense machine-gun power, it banked and passed round the stern. It then flew off north-east in a hail of gunfire. Meanwhile a torpedo had passed along the port side of the *City of Canterbury* and cleared the stern by about 50 feet. Notwithstanding that some of the details do not entirely match, it is likely that this was the attack described by Doyle, the "Marine from Mandalay", whose remarkable story of his escape from Burma after the Japanese victory there, has recently been revealed.[22] Though the *City of Canterbury* escaped unscathed, *Rawnsley* was not so lucky. With a loud explosion, a torpedo struck the supply ship. She slewed 75 degrees off course and was well under water as the survivors were taken off by the cruisers. One of the attacking planes was apparently hit, with smoke seen to be coming from its tail as it rapidly lost height.

The convoy proceeded rapidly to Suda Bay, wary of the suspected presence of German E- and U-boats in the Kaso Straits. No further attacks developed before the arrival at Suda the next morning at 9.30. Three months after leaving the UK, the MNBDO had arrived at its destination. John Havers of Winchester was a sub-lieutenant RNVR, based at Suda Bay at the time with the Sea Transport Service. He recalls that in spite of complete mastery of the air by the *Luftwaffe*, his organisation managed to get the forward end of the *City of Canterbury* alongside the tiny quay to disembark the 1,500 marines. There were neither pilots nor tugs nor boatmen at Suda, and little enough water for a ship the size of the *City of Canterbury*. Nonetheless, the discharge of troops and supplies commenced at once as, according to the Divisional STO, the ship was to sail again in convoy at 5 p.m. with 2,000 Australian and New Zealand troops who had been evacuated from Greece. Although the disembarkation of the MNBDO marines proceeded rapidly, the unloading of guns, transport and equipment proved more time-consuming, as the Australian stevedores, who were really an engineer unit, struggled with huge gun-pulling "Matadors".[23] The last of the cargo was finally unloaded at 1.30 a.m. on Saturday, May 10.

The arrival of the *City of Canterbury* at Suda Bay was greeted warmly by the men of the 234th HAA Bty, a Kent Territorial battery of the 68th HAA Regiment already mentioned. The 234th HAA Bty had travelled from the UK on the *City of Canterbury* in Convoy WS 5A and had disembarked at Port Suez. On about April 27 they sailed to Crete on the *Ulster Prince*. It was while they were on duty on the cliff-tops overlooking Suda Bay that they saw a familiar shape, with her four derricks, sail into the small harbour. Arthur Steele of Filey, who was with the 234th HAA Bty, recalls that a cheer went up and there was much excitement as their link with home had arrived. Exchange visits between the ship's crew and Bty. personnel were made. Sadly, of the

Durban 1942: A British Troopship Revolt

360 gunners who shared No. 2 hold on the ship, just over 100 were soon to be taken prisoner and the remainder killed after the German invasion of the island.

While at the jetty Captain Percival had received many air raid warnings but no bombs were dropped during his ship's stay, although numerous losses had been inflicted on ships in the bay in the preceding and succeeding periods. John Havers considers it a miracle that she was not sunk in the harbour which had seen HMS *York* and the merchantman *Arranbank* go down. At 7 a.m. on the 10th, the *City of Canterbury* moved off the jetty and anchored close to the shore between the "baffles". On the same evening, she embarked an assortment of passengers which "it would be difficult to rival". There were two Greek princesses, the Greek Crown jewels, the UK Consul-General from Athens, and several other consuls with their wives and families. In addition, there were evacuee soldiers from 15 different units and Distressed British Seamen (DBS) from a dozen ships. Among the soldiers who boarded the ship was John Arnott of Edinburgh. He had served in the RASC, attached to the 60th HAA Regiment, and had escaped the Germans in Greece by hiding in the mountains for two or three months with about seven others. Eventually he arrived with companions at an island in the south where he stole a "caique" and sailed for Crete. After two weeks on Crete, he was evacuated on the *City of Canterbury*, which was ironically the very ship on which he had sailed from the UK in WS 5A.

When McGill went ashore at Suda Bay, he was immediately struck by the sight of thousands of troops marching down from the hills behind the village of Suda.

> They looked tired and worn out, some of them had hardly any clothing on; we were informed that they were some of the men evacuated from Greece. They had had no food for several days and were only now being put on ships to take them back to Egypt. When they saw food rations being unloaded from our ship, they made one mad scramble for the cases. I could not help but feel sorry for them; they took nearly everything.

McGill further observed that the island itself was in utter ruins, a result of mass air-raids which came every day. As invasion was expected, women and children were to be evacuated on the ships in the bay. Some of the troops, he noted, refused to embark, saying that they wanted to meet the Germans when they arrived. Hundreds of soldiers were seen lying in caves on the hills, acting as rearguard. They included British, Australian and New Zealand troops, including the MNBDO contingent which the ship had transported from Egypt. The *City of Canterbury* weighed anchor at 6.30 p.m. on May 10 but her departure was delayed by an hour by an air-raid warning. As she left the shores of Crete escorted by the Australian destroyer *Waterhen*, McGill could see the troops on the quayside. There were many tears shed as some were leaving their island perhaps never to return. For the troops on board, they could look forward to their first decent meal for weeks.

The story of the battle for Crete has been told many times.[24] It tells how a gravely underequipped defence force could not resist the overwhelming forces which the Germans had thrown into their paratroop and glider-borne invasion of the island on May 20. It is a story of brave resistance against superior odds, in which severe losses were inflicted on the invaders before the island capitulated. It is also the story of a determined evacuation of Allied troops at the close of the fighting some ten days after the start of the invasion. Corporal E.W. Hill of Coatbridge, one of the marines who arrived at Suda Bay on the *City of Canterbury*, managed to get aboard HMS *Abdiel* on June 1. There were no more ships after that day.

The *City of Canterbury*, with her motley collection of passengers, arrived at Alexandria in the evening of May 12. Over the next few months, she sailed between the Middle East and East and Southern Africa on numerous voyages, dodging air raids in Alexandria and Port Said, reassuring the nervous Lascar crew who had heard lurid tales from their compatriot DBS who had also been evacuated from Crete, and carrying Italian POWs to Durban. The dramas of WS 5A and Crete and the problem leading to the reading of the Riot Act on a previous voyage were now past.

Her arrival at Durban with the Italian POWs on Friday, June 13 meant that she had now chalked up 30,000 miles since entering the Sea Transport Service. Her stay in Durban for almost six weeks allowed ample time for engine repairs and fumigation. On July 22 she sailed with 1,500 coloured South African troops to the Middle East, calling at Aden for six days to ensure that only four personnel ships at a time would be tied up in Suez Bay. This new instruction followed the loss

Durban 1942: A British Troopship Revolt

of the *Georgic* in Suez Bay. Arriving on August 17, she embarked a prisoners' guard of 177 officers and ORs the following day and set sail for Berbera at 5 p.m. On her arrival on the 23rd, she embarked 1,000 Italian POWs and sailed for Mombasa the same day. It was only after reaching the Kenyan port that it was discovered that the main No. 4 bunker was badly on fire. Steps were taken to douse the flames but, as we shall see, spontaneous combustion was to occur on a subsequent occasion, during the dramatic voyage from Durban to Singapore. For the next couple of months, the ship carried Imperial and South African troops between South Africa and the Middle East and since the ministry in London had ordered the ship to dry dock in September, she spent six days undergoing routine repairs in Durban. A further draft of Italian POWs, followed by the transporting of more coloured Union troops to the Middle East, was completed in November and early December 1941. During this period First Officer Hetherington took over temporary command of the vessel, as Percival was hospitalised in Aden with a serious boil. Percival rejoined the ship at Aden on December 27 1941 and found that she had embarked another 1,000 prisoners for Durban.

Chapter 2

Prelude to Mutiny

According to C.B.A. Behrens,[1] the official historian of the merchant navy at war, all the troopship demands of the Allies were in sight of fulfilment by the time of Pearl Harbor. By the beginning of December 1941 the most urgently required troops had been or were being sent to the Indian Ocean area. This region included the Middle East. The situation, needless to say, altered dramatically after December 7 1941. Much of South-East Asia fell quickly to the Japanese. Not only the Western Pacific but also the Indian Ocean came under threat from the Japanese fleet. India, Australia and even the Middle East became vulnerable. "In all the territories immediately menaced, there arose an urgent need for troops and weapons. Large additional numbers of troops were required in India; the Australians demanded the return of two of their divisions from the Middle East".[2] The new situation imposed demands for more cargo vessels to carry military supplies, which would inevitably have a knock-on effect elsewhere. New trooping demands were made. Calcutta became unavailable as a port following the closure of the Bay of Bengal to merchant shipping in March 1942. Repairs to ships had to be effected at Bombay or at South African ports, where Dutch and other merchant vessels scurried to escape the Japanese onslaught on the Dutch East Indies. With naval bases at Singapore and Ceylon no longer available, even more pressure to provide berthing and repair facilities was placed on ports such as Durban.[3] Turnaround time became longer and convoys more difficult to organise and synchronise. While the specific difficulties in Durban will be discussed later, the decision to send troop reinforcements to the Far East shortly after the attack on Pearl Harbor involved the *City of Canterbury* in sailing to a new theatre of war. Assigned to carry RAF personnel and a Royal Army Ordnance Corps (RAOC) company to Singapore from Durban, she was about to become the cause of a protest walk-off of troops which in wartime could have led the protesters before a firing squad.

It is necessary to say something about the organisation of reinforcements for the Far East; about convoy WS 14 which sailed from the UK to South Africa with the servicemen who, on their transfer to the *City of Canterbury*, refused to sail on her; about the port of Durban and about the attractions of Durban city which, as perhaps was the case with the complainants on the voyage to Suez already described, may well have aggravated the sense of deprivation felt by some of the "mutineers".

By January 1 1942 the Chiefs of Staff had laid down the following war aims:

(a) Security of SINGAPORE and of sea communications in the Indian Ocean is [sic] second only to the security of the UNITED KINGDOM and the sea communications thereto.

(b) The defeat of GERMANY must remain our primary object. Consequently for the present we should NOT rpt NOT divert more of our resources than are necessary to hold the Japanese.

(c) CRUSADER [i.e. the Eighth Army's desert campaign in Libya from November 1941 to January 1942] should be exploited to the greatest possible extent subject to the condition that it must NOT rpt NOT prevent despatch of essential reinforcements to the Far East[4]

The War Cabinet accepted the proposals and the decisions cabled to the Commanders-in-Chief Far East, Middle East and India. Wavell, the C-in-C, India, opposed the decision to transfer more of his promised reinforcements to Malaya.[5] In particular, the Chiefs of Staff's refusal to allow any of the 18th British Division to be retained for the defence of Burma and India disappointed him. He had been promised these troops by Churchill. The Chiefs of Staff replied that the situation had now changed dramatically since Churchill's promise. They concluded that the Japanese were much more likely to pursue the capture of the Philippines and of Malaya as a priority, and only subsequently mount a campaign against Burma.[6]

On December 8 1941 the Chiefs of Staff received a telegram sent jointly by the C-in-C, Far East, Lt. Gen. Sir Henry Pownall, and the C-in-C, Eastern Fleet, Sir Geoffrey Layton, which emphasised the importance of air power in defending Northern Malaya. Consequently they agreed to send as much spare capacity as possible from the

Prelude to Mutiny

European theatre. Initially equipment would go to India, whence it would be sent to the Far East. However, following Japanese air attacks in Burma, all reinforcements had to be sent by sea. On December 17 a wing of Hurricane fighters, being carried in convoy round the Cape, was diverted to Singapore 5,000 miles away, along with the pilots and ground staff for one squadron.[7] Even then, they were not immediately available for use on arrival on January 8 1942, as reassembly and testing were required before combat use.[8] Thus the assumption underlying the defence plan for Malaya, that is the rapid deployment of air reinforcements to threatened points, proved false. The arrival of short-range fighters in Malaya would take time. Their assembly and testing would also be time-consuming. Meanwhile existing air power in Malaya, necessary for the additional purpose of keeping open the sea lines of communication, was gradually being dissipated under the weight of Japanese attacks. Basically the Chiefs of Staff were "forced into bolstering up what was already a lost cause".[9] Troop convoys were organised on a hectic scale, with the defence of Java and Sumatra, in conjunction with the Dutch, acknowledged to be essential for the ultimate protection of the Singapore Naval Base.[10] Between January 20 and 27 1942 four convoys were expected to arrive in the Far East, three at Singapore and one, setting out from Sydney, at Oosthaven (Sumatra). Among the reinforcements were the 18th Division (less the 53rd Brigade Group), the 44th Indian Infantry Brigade Group, reinforcements for the Australian 8th Division, an Australian machine-gun battalion, drafts for the 9th and 11th Divisions, one light tank squadron, and five LAA batteries.[11] The *City of Canterbury* was, however, involved with the next two convoys which were scheduled for Singapore in early February. These were convoy BM 12 (Bombay–Singapore) and convoy DM 2 (Durban–Singapore), the latter consisting of drafts sent out from the UK to Durban on December 8 1941 in convoy WS 14D. As we shall see, although the *City of Canterbury* sailed with DM 2 to Singapore, and was joined by the ships of BM 12 after rendezvous off the Maldive Islands, the destination of her sister ships in DM 2 was changed in mid-voyage. *They* would proceed to Batavia (Java) while the *City of Canterbury*, accompanied by the BM 12 ships, would continue to Singapore. While it is questionable whether the vast majority of the servicemen aboard her would have avoided capture by the Japanese had the *City of Canterbury* continued to Batavia with the rest of DM2, the "mutineers" of Durban undoubtedly avoided that fate, though they were scarcely to know that at the time of their protests.

In order to discover the identity of those who sailed or refused to sail on board her from Durban, we have to go back to convoy WS 14. The original terminus for WS 14 was Suez, and among the Army units travelling in the convoy were the 21st LAA Regiment and the 77th HAA Regiment, a Welsh regiment. On December 29 the Chiefs of Staff had decided that these drafts, due to arrive in Durban on January 8, should proceed to Singapore.[12] As to those soldiers who actually sailed on the *City of Canterbury* from Durban, the principal unit (arguably the only Army unit) was a Royal Army Ordnance Corps company, No. 4 Ordnance Store Company (OSC) under the command of Major Robert Peaty, which had travelled out to Durban on the *Highland Princess* and had then transferred to the *City of Canterbury*.

When attempting to identify the units to which the RAF servicemen involved in the *City of Canterbury* affair were attached, there is considerable difficulty. Unlike unit organisation within the Army where soldiers tend to be attached to particular companies throughout their service careers, RAF personnel, particularly ground crew, often found themselves allocated to various units at different times in their careers. Thus labelling them as belonging to particular units is a hazardous exercise. Those RAF ground crew who arrived in Durban from the UK aboard the *Andes* and the *Athlone Castle*, luxurious vessels compared with the *City of Canterbury*, quite simply could not say to which units they were to be allocated. Most of them were skilled craftsmen, such as joiners, engineers and armourers, who would expect to be allocated on arrival to particular units. During the voyage they would know their draft number, but would have no idea as to which unit they would be joining. What is known is that on convoy WS 14, the following units were being shipped to the Far East: No. 266 Wing HQ, less one air commodore, one wing commander, two squadron leaders and one flying officer; No. 242 (Fighter) Squadron, less pilots; No. 258 (Fighter) Squadron, less pilots; No. 605 (Fighter) Squadron, less pilots; No. 47 Embarkation Office; No. 41 Air Stores Park; and No. 62 Repair and Salvage Unit.[13] Together with a pool of 15 pilots who also travelled in WS 14, these accounted for approximately 500 officers, warrant officers, senior NCOs and other ranks.[14] At least that number again (and more) were to be shipped on the *City of Canterbury* from Durban, simply as reinforcements for existing units in the Far East. The difficulty in identification is one which even the C-in-C, Far East had to face. Thus, in responding to the Chiefs of Staff directive of January 1 1942, listing their priority war aims, the C-in-C Far East had cabled on January 6 his own order of preference for reinforcements. The first two on his list were the units and reinforcements in WS 14 and the remainder of 18th Division still in India. He added significantly, "Impossible to state priority which should be given to ancillary units required for formations in [his rank order], since detail of units in WS 14 is NOT rpt NOT yet known".[15] As we shall see, it did not in fact matter. The arrivals were not needed in Singapore as there were few RAF planes left to speak of that they could service and fewer aerodromes left in British hands. The next stop would be Batavia, the story much the same. For most of the ground crews there would be no further destination to which they could escape.

Convoy WS 14 set out from the UK on December 8 1941, with 11 troopships carrying 38,148 troops and 16 other vessels.[16] The mood at the start of the journey was desperately gloomy. Pearl Harbor had been attacked the previous day and news of the sinking of the *Repulse* and the *Prince of Wales* was announced on the wireless as the Glasgow section of the convoy sailed down the Clyde, to rendezvous with the Liverpool portion.[17] The trip itself was uneventful until the convoy reached Freetown, Sierra Leone, where it anchored for a few days. On leaving the swept channel on Christmas Day, an escort vessel reported a distinct echo sounding. Depth charges were dropped but no torpedoes appeared to have been fired. Though the convoy turned away 90° to port for some three-quarters of an hour, the scheduled course was then resumed. On December 27 one of the troopships, the Blue Funnel line *Orestes*, was forced to stop with engine trouble and disappeared from view. She eventually made Cape Town on January 5. On January 3 the *Andes* was sent ahead at speed to enter Cape Town with the vice-president of the South African senate. She rejoined the Durban section of the convoy on January 5. At 1800 hours on January 4 HMS *Ramillies* and two escort vessels proceeded with the Cape Town section, while HMS *Derbyshire* and HMS *Bridgewater* accompanied the Durban section, which arrived in port on January 8.[18]

Congestion at the port of Durban had been the object of trenchant criticism from the C-in-C South Atlantic in October 1941. "It is nothing unusual", he complained, "to have twenty-five ships anchored outside Durban . . . awaiting berths."[19] Troopships going round the Cape to reach Middle Eastern ports (since the Mediterranean was closed to shipping) or leaving South Africa for the Far East; cargo vessels travelling from the Indian Ocean to South Africa and the Middle East; and ships of the Royal Navy all made their demands on the limited resources of the South African port. As Behrens remarks:

> There were not enough drydocks, not enough skilled labour, not enough railway wagons; not enough, indeed, of most of the necessary facilities and provisions, and as the shortages increased, so did the sources of confusion.[20]

The British High Commissioner in South Africa, Lord Harlech, had commented acidly on the shortcomings of British organisation in South African ports. Having visited a number of ports, he noted that:

> It is tragic that, while Durban has been so congested, Port Elizabeth – and East London also – have been so little used by our Ministry of War Transport or by the Royal Navy during the war. The Admiral of Simonstown, who is Principal Sea Transport Officer, has never set foot in either, and his representative at Port Elizabeth struck me as quite inadequate to the opportunity.[21]

Harlech observed that the South African Railway Administration, which owned and ran Port Elizabeth and East London most efficiently, would be willing to develop facilities for the British, if only they were asked. He urged that the PSTO should pay more visits to those ports as well as to Durban, and maintain direct personal contact with the port commandants and port directors appointed for the South African Railway Administration. He concluded that the "fundamental policy should always be, to use every available berth at the subordinate ports all the time to prevent the long waits of ships in the roads outside Durban, waiting turn to enter".

The practice of imposing drastic administrative remedies to counteract confusion and inertia had been applied in the case of Middle East ports in 1941, with the result that the effects of Pearl Harbor were not acutely felt in that region. In respect to India and South Africa, however, wartime reorganisation had not taken place before Japan went to war. At the end of 1941, that is after the international situation had taken a dramatic turn for the worse, the Ministry of War Transport concluded:

Prelude to Mutiny

> It seems . . . clear that effective improvement in the control of ports is bound up with the establishment of a really live Ministry of War Transport organisation . . . and especially with its appropriate articulation, so that responsible people with capacity and power to act are established at the main ports, subject of course, to the final authority of our principal representative . . .[22]

In January 1942 naval complaints were expressed that in the case of convoys leaving from both Cape Town and Durban (which is further east), the Cape Town section had to remain in port after fuelling and provisioning was completed until the date of readiness of the Durban section was known. Moreover, complained the Navy, while WS 14 was at Durban, all Durban-bound traffic from other ports was suspended while Durban tried to cope with 75 sea-going vessels, of which 27 were at outer anchorage. Finally it was pointed out that while diversion of ships in mid-voyage was acceptable, the difficulty arose if transshipment of cargoes was necessary. The loading of troopships should be carried out in such a way as to confine the transshipment of cargoes only to exceptional cases.[23] The Chiefs of Staff did in fact issue instructions on January 8 that personnel and vehicles, sent as reinforcements from the Middle East to the Far East, should be loaded by brigade group so far as possible, to allow any diversions if necessary.[24] Problems abounded, however, in pushing through a radical restructuring of facilities and services in South African ports. There was an independent Union government with whom the British had to negotiate, the clamour and urgency of battle were far distant, the shortages and privations felt in Britain were not experienced in South Africa and, perhaps significantly, the troopships themselves tended not to be unduly held up waiting to dock. For it was recognised that the efficiency of troops as a fighting force depended partly on their fitness. After being couped up on board ship for weeks on end during a voyage, they needed to be active as quickly as possible to renew their energies.

Nonetheless, despite the obstacles, there was a determination on the part of the Ministry of War Transport to push through the organisational changes thought necessary. The ministry commissioned Brigadier N.S. Falla of the Union Steamship Company of New Zealand to travel out to South African ports ostensibly to inspect the ministry organisation in the Union. But, as Lord Harlech, the British High

Commissioner in South Africa pointed out, such an inspection would inevitably have to extend to *Union* organisation; this of course was a much more delicate issue.[25] The South African government was jealous of its autonomy, and proposals for improvement in port organisation had to be sensitive to this aspect. According to Harlech, who had spoken to the South African Minister for Railways (who ran the ports) in November 1941, the Falla visit was welcomed with a view to obtaining practical assistance in securing for South African ports more skilled labour and supervisory staff from the UK. Criticisms of the Union government, it was implied, would have to be muted.

The upshot was that the ministry in London resolved to impress on Falla, prior to his departure:

> ... the importance of not offending the susceptibilities of the Union authorities particularly by any action or expression of views suggesting he was enquiring into matters relating to the Union Government's own organisation, or by putting forward to them any suggestions which might create political difficulties, e.g. any idea of dilution of white by coloured labour, which would raise extremely awkward racial and political questions.[26]

Armed with this advice, Falla visited a number of ports in the region between December 1941 and February 1942. He came away convinced that the South African government were committed to expediting the movement of shipping in their ports, and pointed to a conference in Johannesburg in November, opened by Prime Minister Smuts, as evidence of this intention. Improvements in port organisation and in ship repair facilities were confidently expected as a result.

Falla was also impressed by the diligence and knowledge of the ministry's representative in South and East Africa, Mr. A.M. Campbell, in whom South African officials also appeared to repose great trust. This "personal factor makes for the closest collaboration with Union Authorities with whom he is in harmony", Falla considered. Nonetheless, the appointment of a deputy to Mr. Campbell in Durban would enhance Campbell's status at this important port. Whereas at Middle Eastern ports, the practice existed of holding daily meetings of ministry and "attached" officers, it was felt that:

... under Union Government Administration with its various complexities, daily Meetings along the lines laid down elsewhere involving local port Authorities would be impracticable and by them unacceptable. With all their willingness they have a definite outlook on their own prerogative which it is not wise to disturb.[27]

The "political" implications of reorganisation proposals were thus carefully assessed before recommendations were made. Indeed, as we shall see, the steps taken by the British service authorities to court-martial the Durban protesters were seen by some South Africans as insensitive to the Union's political authority.

While praising the work of the shipping companies' agents – the *City of Canterbury's* South African agents were Ellerman & Bucknall (Pty) Ltd. – and while recognising that on occasion cargo-handling in South African ports might go on all through the night, Falla believed the major deficiency was in the Sea Transport branch of the work, which was under naval administration. Especially at Durban, the ST division was under strength when dealing with the rush of ships arriving in convoy. Imperial Movement Control, organising troops' arrivals and despatches, appeared to possess a better supply of trained personnel, an ironic remark in the light of the events occurring at Durban on January 13. Particular criticism was directed against the over-centralised control exercised by the Admiralty. Thus Falla advised that the offices of PSTO, South Africa, and STO, Durban, be separated from those of Flag Officer, Simonstown, and Naval Liaison Officer (NLO), Durban. In Alexandria, by contrast, the PSTO was a separate officer housed "rightly" in the Ministry of War Transport (MWT) building. Falla concluded that the tendency in South Africa of regarding the STO as primarily a naval rather than a mercantile marine appointee probably stemmed from the pre-1940 practice, before ships were required to reach the Middle East via the Cape. While existing coordination between the MWT and STOs was satisfactory, an improvement could be made by appointing a deputy ministry representative at Durban, as previously recommended.[28]

The proposals, according to Behrens, appear not to have borne immediate fruit. She comments that the appropriate port and transit organisation was not introduced until 1943, by which time, following the reopening of access to Calcutta and the reduction of traffic in the Indian Ocean area, the pressure had diminished. No ministry

Durban 1942: A British Troopship Revolt

trouble-shooter comparable to the appointee in the Middle East had been sent out during the critical periods (presumably, therefore, Campbell and Hankinson could not meet in full the demands of the ministry), and the port of Durban continued to face a backlog of ships waiting to dock and to unload their cargoes. In May and June 1942 an average of 78 ocean-going vessels were tied up in, or lying just outside, South African ports. While Britain consequently waited much longer for essential imports, the exporting countries of the Indian Ocean and the South Pacific had to be supported by Britain at a time when the latter herself was suffering shortages of food, commodities and raw materials.[29]

Having arrived at Durban, what sort of welcome awaited the troops of WS 14, prior to the next stage of their voyage to Singapore aboard the *City of Canterbury*? Durban was a quite stunning city of 262,765 residents, of whom there were 93,313 Europeans, 71,382 Africans (mostly Zulus), 89,806 Indians and 8,264 Cape Coloureds.[30] It was the premier seaport and a popular all-year-round holiday resort for South Africans. The average maximum temperature throughout the year was 76.4 °F. and minimum was 63 °F. In midsummer, that is between December and February, the average maximum temperature was 81.3 °F.

Much of the social life for visiting troops revolved around the various refreshment canteens and clubs in the city, where they might forget for a while the shortages back home. In the central area of Durban there was the Victoria League Canteen in Pine Street (near the GPO and railway station); the Wesley Hall Canteen in West Street; the Navy League Club in Metal Buildings; the SAWAS Canteen in the Old Court House; the Salvation Army Soldiers Red Shield Club, next to the Mayfair Hotel; the YMCA in Beach Walk; the South African Women's Voluntary Air Force Canteen opposite the Mayfair; the Sons of England Rest Room and Canteen in Union Buildings and the TOC H Servicemen's Club in Gardiner Street. In the Beach area there was the Durban Jewish Club in Old Fort Road and the Stand Easy Club in the Pavilion Tea Room. In the Point District on the way to the docks, were to be found St. Peter's Canteen in Point Road, the Seamen's Institute and Rest also in Point Road opposite the Vasco da Gama Clock, and the Missions to Seamen in Wellington Road, the last-named being restricted to seamen.[31] These canteens and clubs offered various kinds of facilities including refreshments and meals, sports, dances, sing-songs and reading and writing materials. The YMCA and Seamen's Institute also provided sleeping accommodation, while cinema shows and concerts were sometimes arranged. Typical charges for refreshments and light meals included tea or coffee at 4d; tea, scone and butter 7d; milk shake 4d and 6d; Coca-Cola 3d; fish and chips with bread and butter and tea or mineral 1s 6d; mixed grill with bread and butter, tea or coffee 2s 6d.

For travelling around Durban, and enjoying its scenery at the same time, servicemen could hire a rickshaw at the authorised rate of 6d per mile or portion thereof. Alternatively, the trolley bus service was popular. Gerald Townsend from Swindon, a sergeant in the Royal Signals, arrived in Durban in WS 14 aboard the appropriately named *Durban Castle*, and recalls seeing the trolley cars loaded to the doors with soldiers returning to the docks. Many servicemen were hanging on precariously to the outsides of the buses. A special train service ran between the city and Clairwood Transit Camp.

Writing in a Durban magazine, the *Forum*, a local journalist drew his readers' attention to a new malady, the "Convoy Blues",[32] which afflicted the city once a convoy had left. At first, he wrote:

> ... the City was shy of these hordes of pink-and-white strangers with clumsy turned-up shorts and overlarge topees that made them look like *Punch* caricatures of Tommies in tropical Kit".

But the ice soon broke and the city, "especially its women folk", took these visitors into their hearts. An atmosphere of expectation was created when a convoy was due (though, with censorship restrictions, no one really knew until it had arrived):

> And then up from Point Road and Maydon Wharf begins that now familiar and welcome clump, clump, clump of heavy army boots, as like a swarm of friendly locusts the "Imperials" descend on the City.

Pte. Alfred Evans of No. 4 OSC, bunking on the *Andes* prior to his transfer to the *City of Canterbury*, confided in his diary that for five days he and his colleagues were able to "hit the town each day. It was great".[33] Fruits, mangoes, bananas and chocolate bars were freely available, a delight to those used to rationing of basic foods back home. In the five days available Evans had time to visit most of Durban, parts of Natal Province, the Umbilo River, the Valley of a Thousand Hills, and to admire the monkeys roaming free. He went to concerts and danced at the South Africa Victory League Club. A rickshaw race along the seafront, being pulled by powerful Zulus in traditional costume, would be followed by bathing in the large breakers rolling in from the sea. And then transfer to the *City of Canterbury*.

For Leading Aircraftman F.C. Welding, one of the Durban "mutineers", his first impression on arrival was of the intense dry heat after the cool sea breezes and long voyage.[34] Wishing to experience on his own the sensation of stepping off his ship on to foreign soil, he slipped away ahead of his companions. He remembers that:

> ... as I stepped off the gangway, I felt the hot dry sand of the dockside straight through the soles of my shoes. Just outside the Dock gates an old negro man and two small children were sitting on a doorstep watching us, and it was then that I really felt, "Now I am in Africa." The excitement of the moment was one that I had never felt before or since.

On his first trip into the city itself, he saw a long line of African prisoners chained together, working on road repairing and being guarded by white prison officers with guns. He and his colleagues then went to an Indian-run cafe and ordered eggs and chips: "The waiter said, 'How many eggs you want, sir?' an incredible question to us as eggs had been rationed in England to one a week".

The sights of Durban were apparently appreciated with great relish by the Australian troops en route to the Middle East in 1941. Mr. L. Peterson of York, an RNR petty officer who had arrived in Durban aboard the *Empress of Canada* on his way to Alexandria, vividly remembers the antics of the Australians. They commandeered the brewery dray horses and conducted races with them through the Durban streets. The police on points duty were stripped of their uniforms. They also took over the rickshaws, sat the rickshaw boys in the seats and took over the pulling themselves, journeying to the nearest pub. The prohibition on the boys being allowed into the pubs was of course ignored by the Aussies. At night cars were stolen. Indeed so taken with the country were some of the visiting troops that desertion to the goldfields was not unknown. Many British servicemen resolved there and then to settle in the country once the war was over.

There were, however, two main highlights of the stopover in Durban. The first was the spectacle of Perla Gibson, the "Lady in White" singing

Prelude to Mutiny

to the troops on their arrival in convoy. Her rendering of "Land of Hope and Glory" is firmly implanted in the memories of thousands of servicemen arriving at Point Docks, including that of John B. Maxwell of Gretna who sailed on the *City of Canterbury* in January 1943 with the 101st LAA Regiment, bound for Bombay. A memorial to her stands on the pier where she sang her patriotic songs.[35]

The other highlight for the troops was to be invited by a local family for a meal and entertainment; even, in some cases, for overnight stays, so long as the troops were back for roll-call the next morning. Doryn Pote of Durban recalls her family offering hospitality to visiting servicemen at their beach cottage at Isipingo Beach, a few miles from the city. At Pingo SAWAS ran a canteen, providing tea at 1d, and cakes and buns also 1d each. Swimming parties would be marched down from Clairwood Transit Camp, and as the South African life-savers had joined the Union forces, youngsters like Doryn Pote would be kept busy watching out for any British troops in difficulty, as many of them could not swim. Doryn Pote's mother ran a first-aid post to patch up the servicemen who had cut themselves on the rocks. One of the young servicemen to whom Doryn's family had offered hospitality was an RAF man on the *City of Canterbury*, though his name cannot now be recalled. Other servicemen recall South African hospitality vividly. The late Hugh Preston from Penrith, an AC2 at the time, wrote in his diary that on January 10 1942 he met a Mr. Pearson from Whitehaven and that the latter took him and his companions to his bungalow at Escombe, where the visitors spent a pleasant afternoon and evening with Mr. and Mrs. Pearson and their two daughters.[36] The following day he met a Mr. Tripp on the beach and once more was invited home to meet the host's family, an invitation repeated for the following day. He and his RAF companions were then driven back to the docks in the Tripps' car and boarded the *City of Canterbury*.

Hugh Preston's experience of being invited to the home of someone who originated in the same part of the UK as his guests was apparently fairly common. Mr. T. Scollan of Droitwich Spa, who sailed on the *Highland Brigade* to Durban, en route to Port Tewfik, Egypt, in mid-1941, recalls being invited to the home of a Mr. and Mrs. Anderson. The husband was a retired station-master but had been recalled to help out during the war. Their son was a lieutenant in the Durban Scottish Regiment and their daughter helped out at the YMCA. Mr. Scollan remembers that they kept a visitors book in which the guest's address, as well as his name, could be inserted. The Andersons would then write to the serviceman's next-of-kin with news of the latter's son or husband, as the case might be, while the serviceman was steaming in convoy for a new destination.

For most convoy troops, part of their time in Durban would be spent billeted at Clairwood Camp, four miles from the city, while waiting for the next convoy or section of convoy to form up. Clairwood, formally known at Imperial Forces Trans-shipment Camp (IFTC), was situated to the south of Durban, overlooking Clairwood Racecourse. It is now an industrial estate, but some of the original buildings are still in existence. During the war it was a huge tented camp, with visiting troops being housed in Bell tents, six occupants to a tent. A section of the camp was allotted for the use of RAF personnel, the administration of which was in the hands of RAF permanent staff.[37] Numbers of airmen in transit, including officers, would range from 4,000 to 15,000 during peak periods. In the period May to July 1942, the monthly average of RAF movements was over 17,000, not including additional movements caused by break-downs of ships. The RAF Liaison Mission in South Africa was critical of the use of transit personnel for administrative duties, basically because, with few exceptions, officers showed "an entire lack of interest in the camp and the RAF personnel attached. In fact, their employment is responsible for a great deal of trouble and error". The nature of this "trouble and error" is not spelled out in the report and it is not at all clear that it relates in any way to the organisational confusion exposed in the wake of the *City of Canterbury* affair.

Ken Lawrence of Sea Park, Natal, who served in the Royal Navy during the war, recalls that in 1943 the humidity was intense in the early part of the year, making living conditions in the tents uncomfortable. When it rained the tents filled up with squelched mud, as the camp was on a slight incline. Other servicemen recall the camp with affection. Mr. A.E. Wheeler of Dyfed, who was with the RAFVR, found the conditions in the period March to April 1942 "quite excellent . . .; after two years in the Sudan and W. Desert, it all seemed like a holiday to me". Gordon Thomas of Park Rynie, Natal, was a newly commissioned Indian Army officer in the 15th Punjab Regiment, when he stayed about a week at Clairwood in February 1942. "The conditions were so pleasant after wartime Britain that even now, 40 years later, when driving past the camp site, I recall with pleasure my short stay there."

A more detailed description of the camp is provided by Ernest Carboni of Durban, a corporal in the 1st Battalion of the Royal Durban Light Infantry, who served on the permanent staff at Clairwood from January 1943 to June 1944. In addition to the line-upon-line of tents, the buildings on site included Montgomery Hall and Tedder Hall. These were messes containing stages for impromptu shows mounted by the troops themselves. The messes served beer but not spirits, unless one had access to the officers' or warrant officers' messes, which were fully-licensed. The Imperial permanent staff under the Camp Commandant, Colonel H.A. Stewart DSO, OBE, were housed in bungalows in the camp, while all Union permanent staff lived in Durban, travelling by train into camp daily and alighting at Merebank Station. Lights out at the camp was officially 2200 hours. In fact, it was common practice for transit troops to stay overnight at Durban and to sneak into camp, under the wire, in time for roll-call at 0900 hours.

There are no available war diaries for the camp covering the period of the *City of Canterbury* incident, when the "mutineers" were housed at the camp under open arrest pending court-martial. War diaries from September 1942 onwards record extremely routine information relating to such matters as alerts and the "all-clear" following reports of enemy submarines or enemy aircraft in the vicinity, usually without incident.[38] They record arrivals and departures of drafts, for example the arrival of over 8,000 officers and men, ex-WS 22, on September 29 1942, and they note the arrival of significant visitors, including Brigadier A.G. Salisbury-Jones, commanding 203 UK Military Liaison Mission, Pretoria, and Air Vice-Marshal M.B. Frew, of the UK Air Ministry Mission, Pretoria.

Following clearance from the Union government, proposals to extend the camp to enable it to accommodate 30,000 troops were approved in the autumn of 1942. The construction of a sewer at no cost to the Imperial government removed one obstacle to its expansion. Hygiene was naturally a major concern of the camp administration, and sewerage construction in place of pit latrines would minimise the threat of disease and help to contain the fly population. As it was usual to find that troops arriving at the camp after a long convoy journey tended to indulge in excessive eating of fruit, which often led in time to diarrhoea and sometimes admission to hospital, the improvement in sanitation conditions was timely. While much of the day for the troops awaiting trans-shipment was in fact spent sightseeing, some training routines were nonetheless followed: these included shooting parties and construction parties, but shortages of ammunition and equipment restricted such activities.

One activity which had to be rehearsed, however, was the camp's emergency scheme.[39] The instructions issued by the security officer in July 1942 warned that, after Pearl Harbor, the enemy might attempt a similar attack on Durban and that enemy units capable of such an attack were known to be in the vicinity (in fact, sabotage by Afrikaaner elements in South Africa was more a potential threat to Union and Imperial forces). The defence of Durban was the responsibility of the Fortress Commander, Union Defence Force, and all Imperial troops at Clairwood were placed at his disposal and would come under his command if called upon. The troops staying at Clairwood were, therefore, organised into four sections. Section A, the permanent AA defence, was recruited from the camp's permanent staff. Section B, the Guard Troops, was found from the Imperial transit troops. They were detailed daily on a half-hour's notice to parade fully armed and equipped in battle order. Their role was to prevent sabotage. Section C, the Reserve Troops, was also made up from the Imperial transit forces. They would be formed into complete units as they returned to camp after an alarm had been sounded. They would provide a striking force under the Fortress Commander. Finally, there was Section D, Passive Troops, that is, all the remaining unarmed Imperial troops whose function was fire-fighting and similar roles.

The Guard Troops were 10 per cent of the total rifle strength in camp each day and were on duty for 24 hours from 1200 hrs to 1200 hrs. They were, in turn, divided into Jayforce, Britforce and Clairforce. Jayforce and Britforce each had one captain, one subaltern, one NCO and approximately two platoons of about 30 ORs each. Clairforce comprised the balance of the 10 per cent rifle strength of the camp after provision had been made for Jayforce and Britforce.

In the event of a general emergency, Jayforce and Britforce were to move out in transports; Clairforce was to "stand to" in the racecourse, awaiting orders; all ranks were to return to the camp immediately by designated routes (no trains would be running); and arms would be

Prelude to Mutiny

issued to the men as they returned.

If there was an air raid alert, the three forces were to parade with their arms in battle order, but remain in readiness. Ten ORs from Clairforce, trained in bren gun handling, would report for orders to the guardroom. Unit commanders would issue rifles to those in camp forming the Reserve Troops, and the remaining troops would take no action. Finally, it was decided that:

> Officers and ORs outside the Camp may remain in any place of entertainment while setting an example to the civil Native population. Those who wish may return to Camp and TRAINS WILL BE RUNNING.

Life in Clairwood, by most accounts, was idyllic. The enemy seemed as far away as Blighty. Having arrived on January 8 1942 after their long sea voyage in relative luxury aboard either the *Andes* or the *Athlone Castle*, and after an enjoyable interlude in the benign environment of Clairwood Camp and the eye-opening splendour of Durban and its beaches, about 1,300 RAF ground crew, a clutch of Australian, British and Canadian sergeant-pilots, a handful of naval personnel and the men of No. 4 Ordnance Store Company, RAOC, boarded the *City of Canterbury* on January 12 1942. Their new conditions were to appal them and to prompt 200 of them to refuse to sail in her.

Chapter 3

Mutiny or Protest?

From various sources, we can build up a picture of how the authorities regarded the events at Point Docks, Durban on January 13 1942. Particularly useful are two signals sent by Air Commodore (later Air Vice-Marshal) M.B. Frew, head of the British Air Ministry Mission, Pretoria, shortly after the incident. The first signal was a telex to the Senior Naval Officer, Simonstown, probably sent on the 14th. The second signal was sent by Frew to the Air Ministry in London and received at Kingsway at 0150 hours on the 16th. Additionally a lengthy report of the subsequent court-martial proceedings, submitted by the Deputy Judge Advocate General (DJAG), Wing Commander (later Group Captain) H.M. Shurlock, who was posted to Durban from Southern Rhodesia in order to take charge of the court proceedings, also spelled out the events at the port.[1] Finally we have a briefer report from Captain Percival, the master of the *City of Canterbury*, which he sent a month after the incident to his employers, the City Line Ltd., at their wartime registered offices at the Woodbank Hotel, Balloch, Dunbartonshire (at the foot of Loch Lomond).

Having examined these accounts of the affair, we shall then turn to the "mutineers" themselves and also to those servicemen who, having walked off the ship in protest, eventually rejoined her before she sailed. While no *sharp* divisions emerge between the "official" and "unofficial" view, there are nonetheless differences of emphasis in the various reconstructions of the events.

As stated in a previous chapter, a large number of troops, both military and RAF, had arrived in Durban on various troopships of convoy WS 14. A number of those who had arrived on January 8 1942 on board the *Andes* and the *Athlone Castle* from the UK, were trans-shipped on January 12 to the *City of Canterbury*. This much smaller and less stylish vessel had sailed from Aden to Durban on December 27 1941, arriving on 7 January with 150 Union troops and 1,000 Italian prisoners-of-war.² After disembarking her passengers, she was made ready for her next voyage as part of a large convoy for Singapore, then engaged in a desperate struggle to prevent the Japanese, already gradually moving south through Malaya, from capturing the island and its crucial naval base.

The service staffing complement for the *City of Canterbury* included the following.³ OC Troops was Wing Commander Kercher DSO, a somewhat remote figure. The adjutant was F/Lt. Joliffe, a reservist from the Isle of Wight. Warrant Officer Brinton had responsibilities for discipline. F/Sgt. A.P. Wheway was in charge of records, and medical staff included F/Sgt. Andrews and AC McCarthy. All had sailed to Durban on the *Cameronia* (Anchor Line, 17,000 tons) in WS 14, travelling with the officers in charge of the ground crews who, like them, were to be assigned to the *City of Canterbury*.

Part of her preparation involved the employment of a gang of "Akitts" to clean all decks thoroughly after the departure of the POWs, even though, as Captain Percival himself wrote to his employers on February 18, the prisoners had left the mess decks in very good order.⁴ Nonetheless, one foreman and 35 boys were hired from January 8 to January 11 inclusive to clean the mess decks, ablution houses and latrines, the work being efficiently completed at a cost of £66. This work was closely supervised by the troops officer and on Friday, January 9, the ship was inspected by a Lt-Cdr., RNR, assistant Sea Transport Officer, during the cleaning operations.⁵ He declared himself satisfied that the work was progressing satisfactorily and that the ship would be ready for embarkation of the RAF and Army personnel on the 12th. One can see immediately why Captain Percival vigorously rejected allegations by the servicemen that he was running an unclean ship.

Another stage in the ship's preparation for her Singapore voyage was to restock her coal bunkers. On the morning of January 8 she consequently moved to the coaling tips at the Bluff in order to shift 300 tons of heated coal from her No. 4 lower bunker to shelter decks, and to take on board 2,300 tons of fresh coal. The ship remained at the Bluff until Sunday morning, January 11, and during these three nights and days, the coal dust from five ships bunkering at the same wharf settled on her. She moved back to the main wharf with coal still on her upper decks and finished mooring at 8 a.m.

Mutiny or Protest?

At 8.30 a.m. the small naval draft commenced to embark and it soon began raining, with the result that the coal dust from the deck and the mud from the wharfs were carried down to the mess decks by the men boarding the ship. The following day embarkation continued, with the RAF and Army personnel climbing on board.

The *City of Canterbury* was not due to sail till the following day, Tuesday, January 13. All the troops aboard her were given shore leave until midnight, even though a large number of the RAF personnel had not yet drawn hammocks, nor familiarised themselves with the lay-out of the ship. Most of them had returned by midnight but according to W/Cdr. Shurlock, in his report of the affair to the Judge Advocate General in London, Sir Harry MacGeagh, some 300 to 400 had not reboarded the ship.[6] Percival thought that the returnees were rather the worse for drink, while Shurlock reported that, "there was a certain amount of riotous behaviour amongst them in the dock area". Complaints were voiced that the ship was dirty, bug-infested, lousy, old and unseaworthy, and lacking life-saving apparatus and sufficient lifebelts in good condition. No doubt as tiredness set in the rioting ceased, and by 0400 hours, the absentees had turned up and spent the night aboard the ship. The next morning the angry demeanour of the men became more marked. Sentries were placed on the gangways, but the men left the ship as and when they pleased. By about 1100 hours, Shurlock added, there were some 300 to 400 men still on the dockside protesting that they were refusing to sail on her.

At 1200 hours, Air Commodore Frew, who had been paying an inspection visit to Durban, was asked by the Officer Commanding Natal Command, Brigadier Daniel, to go to the docks.[7] Accompanied by Captain Black (probably an Imperial Army representative), he found 500 to 600 men standing on the dock. He then collected five Army personnel and five RAF personnel and asked them about their complaints. He proceeded to board the ship himself and inspected the quarters of the Other Ranks. This confirmed that in his opinion, the ventilation was inadequate, though it was pointed out that nothing could be done about it. As to the latrine accommodation, this also was inadequate and – horror of horrors – the Other Ranks' latrines were also being used by the coloured crew members. He immediately ordered that the latrines be reserved for white troops. The lifebelts on the ORs' mess decks were confirmed as being in a very dirty condition, and many were unusable either because the corks had burst out of the cloth or because they were missing the tying cords. However, Captain Percival assured him that he had a sufficient number of serviceable lifebelts for each passenger, though Frew pointed out that they were certainly not available in the men's quarters. The mess decks themselves were rather odorous, while the accommodation was extremely cramped; it was impossible to sling hammocks without them touching each other. More seriously, several of the men on board showed Frew the bites they had received the previous night, and when he dug between boards and pillars in the men's quarters, he found lice, bugs, mosquitoes and other vermin.

The inspection over, Frew addressed the men on the dock and told them he would make an official complaint concerning the condition of the ship, but that the servicemen must go on board her. Otherwise they would be charged with mutiny or desertion and be given severe sentences. He promised that the same state of affairs would not happen again and succeeded in persuading, with the assistance of other officers, 60–70 per cent of those on the dockside to board the ship. That still left perhaps 300 RAF personnel and soldiers who remained adamant in their refusal to board the *City of Canterbury*, though the numbers fell to 160 airmen and 28 soldiers when the ship cast off. It seems that at this point, about 1320 hours, Frew sent a message to the Naval Liaison Officer and Senior Sea Transport Officer at Durban, Captain Nash RN, to come and look at the ship. Located in the Durban Club where he was having his lunch, Nash regretted that he could not oblige. The ship was due to sail at 1430 and Nash replied that he hoped that the mutineers would be suitably dealt with. Frew felt that if Nash had appeared and if the ship had been delayed for a few minutes more most, if not all, of the 188 men would eventually have gone on board. In the event, when the ship did set sail (there are differences of opinion as to whether she sailed on time or 15 minutes late – she had of course to keep a rendezvous at sea), the remaining troops left at the quayside appeared to engage in what Shurlock called a "sit-down strike". Some time later, transport was obtained to take these men to the Imperial Forces Transit Camp, Clairwood, and after considerable delay, their names were taken. According to Shurlock, during this period it would have been quite simple for men either to leave this party or to join it.

It is quite evident that Frew's attitude was remarkably sympathetic.

Mutiny or Protest?

Thus he signalled to the Air Ministry that although there was no justification for the men's refusal to sail, he nonetheless considered that the ship was in an unclean state. The fact that on the two previous voyages the ship had carried coloured native troops and Italian POWs seemed to him to explain her repellent condition, a view which might have reflected contemporary assumptions and prejudices among many whites, British or otherwise, living in South Africa. He concluded by observing that if the ship had been fumigated and cleared of vermin, he was sure that no trouble would have erupted with either the Army or RAF personnel. Indeed, he added in his cypher to the Air Ministry in London, this was a view shared by the Imperial Army, RAF and South African officers who accompanied him on his inspection.

In a similar fashion, the deputy head of No. 203 British Military Mission in South Africa, Colonel C.T. Goldsmith, signalled to the War Office on January 16 that conditions on board the ship were most unsatisfactory. In particular, Goldsmith stressed that those placed under arrest, that is, one Army sergeant, 27 Army ORs, one RAF sergeant and 159 RAF ORs:

> APPEAR IN GENERAL TO BE YOUNG AND INEXPERIENCED PERSONNEL WHOSE SOLE GRIEVANCE WAS CONDITION OF SHIP AND WHO HAVE NO (REPEAT NO) INTENTION TO EVADE SERVICE.[8]

Captain Percival, needless to say, was indignant at these accusations, particularly since an assistant STO had checked the work of the gang of cleaners hired by him before the troops boarded the vessel. The ship's log for that fateful January 13 states that the decks had also been inspected by an Air Force staff officer, with the ship's adjutant and troops officer present.[9] All had expressed themselves satisfied with the cleanliness of the decks. None of the ship's officers had seen any lice or bugs on her, nor had any previously been reported. When the accusations had first been made, officers went to No. 7 mess from where the reports had emanated but could find only a few small cockroaches indigenous to Eastern ships. It was conceded, however, that many of the ship's crew had been bitten by mosquitoes during their stay in Durban.

There was, nevertheless, a further rebuttal by Percival. Whereas Air Commodore Frew felt that the ship ought to have been fumigated, Percival pointed out both in his log and in his report to the ship's

Durban 1942: A British Troopship Revolt

owners that she had been thoroughly fumigated on June 30 1941 and again on November 16 1941 by the Port Health Authority at Durban. "On both these occasions, a double dose of cyanide was used". In the absence of proof (though Frew did, literally, turn up the nauseating evidence), Percival point-blank refused to accept the accusations. His ship, he insisted, was in a "sweet and clean condition" when the troops embarked (indeed, the wharf mud and damp coal dust were spread round the decks by the troops on boarding). The complaints that the ship was old and unseaworthy and lacked adequate life-saving equipment were "too infantile to merit a reply" (though an air commodore had endorsed the expressions of concern). His log for January 13 ended with a plea:

> I hereby protest against such an accusation being levied against a hard working Sea Transport Ship whose officers and staff have done their utmost to maintain an efficient and well ordered ship under conditions which have been unusual and difficult.

The log for that day was signed by Percival, by Joe Hetherington (Mate and First Officer), by T. Macpherson (Purser), by P. Morrison (Troop Officer), and witnessed by T. Innes (Third Mate). As for those who levelled criticism against his ship, they were, he told his employers, "dirty, untidy and undisciplined".

The immediate handling of the affair by the officers present on the quayside drew criticism from DJAG Shurlock in his later report to Sir Harry MacGeagh, the JAG. In particular, Shurlock felt strongly that at the time when the ship was due to sail, and when the 188 personnel had still not been persuaded to go on board, the need for "more drastic action" then arose. "In my opinion", he wrote, "the men should have been 'fallen in', marched to the gangway by an officer, and the names of any men who failed to carry out such order would have been taken on the spot and subsequently arrested and charged". Despite the fact that a number of senior officers were in the vicinity, no such steps were taken. According to Shurlock, it was possible that such officers thought that more drastic action of this nature might produce worse results. But in his opinion, once persuasion had failed, the more robust handling of the incident would have prevented the necessity for the subsequent courts-martial. As we shall see, it was argued by the RAF Embarkation Officer at Durban, Squadron Leader T.J. Erskine, that he *did* give an

Mutiny or Protest?

order to embark, which was collectively ignored (on the basis of this assertion, the capital charge of "joining in a mutiny" was levied against the men, but at the first court-martial the court was to place no reliance on Erskine's evidence).

According to Shurlock, he had discovered through conversation that there were at least four ships which frequently visited Durban and which enjoyed a poor reputation in respect to their condition. Yet in spite of this apparent common knowledge, he could discover no-one, nor hear of any steps which were ever taken, to improve these conditions. There appeared to be no-one with the necessary authority, initiative or ability to rectify the situation. Echoing the prejudices of the age, Shurlock, like Frew, also commented on the alleged consequences of transporting "native" troops and POWs on the ship's previous voyages. For it did not, "require much imagination on the part of anyone with war experience" to realise that it was "highly probable" that a ship used for such purposes, would be in a "very dirty and verminous condition". Between her docking at Durban on January 7 and her departure on January 13, nothing had been done, he stated, somewhat misleadingly, to disinfect or to fumigate the ship. Her last fumigation, he asserted in contradiction to Percival, had been in September 1941. It was true, conceded Shurlock, that the Port Health Office's representative had examined the ship on her arrival and had certified her as being fit for further Sea Transport service. But, "It is needless to point out that very little reliance could be placed on his certification".

The Port Health Officer whose report to the SNO at Simonstown had been transmitted to the Admiralty, recounted the history of the ship's previous fumigation in November 1941.[10] Apparently, certain of the naval draft in a previous voyage had complained to the OC draft that they had been bitten by mosquitoes and, as a result, the ship had been fumigated. As to the immediate incident in January, it was conceded that no proper preliminary inspection as laid down in King's Regulations had been carried out. Owing to the rush of work, it was impossible to collect all the officers concerned at any one time (the congestion at Durban, as we have seen, was appalling). The OC Troops (Wing Commander Kercher) did, however, inspect the troop decks and latrines and reported they were clean and adequate and that therefore the ship was fit to receive troops. The latrines, he added, were designed for the use of 1,527 men, whereas only 1,350 were to be embarked, thus

Durban 1942: A British Troopship Revolt

avoiding overcrowding. To allay sensitivities, separate latrine facilities for the Lascar crew members were to be maintained.

It was later also pointed out by Air Vice-Marshal Grahame (later Sir Grahame) Donald, Deputy Air Member for Supply and Organisation (D/AMSO) at the Air Ministry, that a permanent military senior medical officer had been aboard the ship and had not reported adversely on the health risks posed by her condition.[11] The health of the (native) troops previously on board the *City of Canterbury* had been good, hygiene and sanitation had been maintained and no cases of infectious diseases had occurred. The nub of the matter, minuted Donald, was that, "most of the trouble is due to the fact that the personnel in question trans-shipped [sic] at Durban from the *Athlone Castle* [Shurlock also cited the *Andes*] which is a much more modern and comfortable vessel than the *City of Canterbury*. The sharp difference in standards of comfort gave the men a prejudiced view of the *City of Canterbury*". As Wing Commander C.J. Salmon, in the Deputy Director of Movements branch, reported to Donald, the incident was, "further proof that our personnel must be educated regarding trooping problems before leaving this country [UK], and much is now being done to attain this aim".[12]

We can leave the organizational and administrative fall-out of the incident to Chapter Five and revert to the situation of the "mutineers". As we saw previously, they had been transported to IFTC, Clairwood, where they were first placed in the charge of Flight Lieutenant D. Bradley, another officer who failed to impress W/Cdr. Shurlock. The latter had alluded to the difficulty of identifying just who the "refuseniks" were and from which units they had been drawn. No witnesses could identify with certainty *any* man in the party. All documents in respect to them, to their units and to their destination had gone with the ship. Their officers had also sailed. Unlike the army personnel who belonged only to one unit, the RAF personnel were all reinforcements of various kinds, whose duties could not be discovered from a single source. When they arrived at Clairwood, the men were without their kit, which was still aboard the ship. Yet according to Shurlock, Bradley had told him that the men had not in fact been issued with any kit at the camp. This statement was shown at the subsequent court-martial to be false and, in Shurlock's view, was a deliberate attempt by Bradley to mislead him in order to protect the men from being identified as part of the *City of Canterbury* draft. Bradley had recently been promoted from Warrant Officer and was clearly "on the side of the men". As such, Shurlock considered him unsuitable for his post, and recommended his transfer.

A further irritant for Shurlock was the absence of the assistant Provost-Marshal (APM), the officer whom Shurlock considered was pivotal in matters of this kind. As he ruefully reported, "It was somewhat disquieting to learn on arrival at Durban where I had proceeded with all possible haste, that this officer had left for Cape Town. I do not know by whose orders". Shurlock concluded that the APM in question appeared to have very little knowledge of matters connected with his appointment and that his experience of courts-martial was minimal. Shurlock acknowledged the difficult tasks facing the APM in Durban who dealt with large numbers of troops in transit either to or from a theatre of war. For such personnel, after spending a long period at sea, were inclined to "enjoy the amenities of Durban and the hospitality of the South African people". As with other officers in this affair, the APM apparently failed to meet the exacting standards which Shurlock considered appropriate and was also recommended for replacement.

So with nearly 200 recalcitrant army and RAF servicemen unexpectedly deposited at Clairwood, the authorities now considered the possible disciplinary steps to be taken against them. A flurry of signals flew back and forth across three continents. Brigadier Salisbury-Jones, head of the Military Mission in Pretoria, wired the War Office on January 16 with the possible alternatives. These were either to court-martial all those who refused to embark on the *City of Canterbury*; or to take a more lenient view of the ORs by dealing with them summarily, while trying the NCOs by court-martial. There was also a third possibility which Salisbury-Jones had discussed with his deputy, Col. Goldsmith on January 14.[13] That was simply to send on all the arrestees to their destination. The views of the War Office were urgently sought on those alternatives, though Salisbury-Jones felt that:

> TROOP REQUIREMENTS MAY OUTWEIGH DISCIPLINARY ASPECT. WOULD HOWEVER POINT OUT THAT FUTURE OCCURRENCES MUST (REPEAT) MUST BE AVOIDED AND ALL TROOPS DESTINED FOR OVERSEAS IN FUTURE WARNED TO EXPECT ABNORMAL CONDITIONS.[14]

Durban 1942: A British Troopship Revolt

At the Air Ministry in London, Frew's signal of January 14 was surprisingly not yet to hand, but the ministry had received, through the War Office, Salisbury-Jones' signal of January 16. Babington, the AMP, wired back to Frew on the 17th:

> VERY SERIOUS VIEW TAKEN OF OFFENCES AND PERSONNEL INVOLVED ARE TO BE TRIED BY COURT-MARTIAL.

A further signal to Shurlock in Southern Rhodesia requested that he "ADVISE ON SERIOUS CASE OF MUTINY", but complicating this concern for discipline was the critical situation in the Far East which was naturally dominating the minds of the senior officers in the services. Thus Babington, in his signal to Pretoria of January 17, stated that once they had been court-martialled, the personnel involved were to proceed to their destination in the Far East by the first available transport, which was thought would be around February 11. In the event of a conviction, the confirming officer should consider the suspension of sentences to enable the men to travel onwards to Singapore where they were urgently needed. On the 19th, a signal from Air HQ, Far East, stated tersely:

> AS PERSONNEL URGENTLY REQUIRED SUGGEST THAT NCOS AND RING LEADERS BE COURT-MARTIALLED AND REMAINDER SENT ON HERE ASAP.

Field general courts-martial, a speedier way of proceeding than by general courts-martial, were set down to commence on January 29, when the first batch of 30 RAF men would be tried. A number of legal difficulties had to be overcome in the first instance before the proceedings, against the RAF men in particular, could be considered regular. The legal problems stemmed from the fact that the alleged offences took place in South Africa where the jurisdiction of the UK's Air Force Act had to be established, and could not be assumed. The Pretoria Military Mission, which admittedly could hardly speak with authority on Air Force law, had ventured the opinion that:

> RAF IN SOUTH AFRICA ARE NOT (REPEAT) NOT SUBJECT TO AIR FORCE ACT BUT TO UNION DISCIPLINE CODE AND COMPOSITION OF RAF COURT MAY OFFER DIFFICULTIES.

Mutiny or Protest?

Though Air Commodore Frew apparently agreed with this interpretation, Babington had no doubts on the matter:

> RAF PERSONNEL INVOLVED ARE (REPEAT) ARE CONSIDERED TO HAVE BEEN SUBJECT TO AIR FORCE LAW AT TIME OF ALLEGED OFFENCE. VIDE A.M.O. [AIR MINISTRY ORDER] A.373/41.

Shurlock, the DJAG, had also anticipated legal difficulties in respect to the RAF men. He agreed that the alleged offences had been committed under Air Force law but the military control of Clairwood Camp, where the RAF personnel were being held, could also present jurisdictional problems. The difficulty was neatly sidestepped by the expedient of creating a new RAF detachment, No. 2 RAF Detachment, Durban, to which all the dispersed personnel were transferred. Shurlock was also able to secure W/Cdr. R.F. Shenton, who was in transit in Durban, to command the instantly created unit and, in accordance with Air Force law, Shenton became the convening officer (i.e. the empanelling officer) for the courts-martial. The detachment perhaps constituted the only instance when virtually 100 per cent of those in a unit were court-martialled (one serviceman was not tried because of illness).

The JAG in London, Sir Harry MacGeagh, was not wholly convinced of the correctness of this procedure. In a report to Babington, the AMP, in May 1942, he advised that only if the Air Council were satisfied on a number of points, would the courts-martial be legally in order.[15] These were that there was authority, properly granted, to form No. 2 Detachment, to make the accused members of that unit, and that W/Cdr. Shenton was properly in command of it. In this instance, McGeagh felt that this was a matter for the "Air Force authorities". The Director of Personal Services (DPS), Air Commodore (later Air Vice-Marshal) Arthur Fiddament, later explained, in a memorandum to the AMP, the intricacies of the procedure adopted.[16] First, he pointed out that directions given by the Air and Army Councils (in AMO A. 1086/41 and the parallel Army Council Instruction [ACI]) declared that every officer and airman of the regular Air Force, serving in a transit camp administered by the Military Authorities (such as the IFTC at Clairwood), should be temporarily attached to the regular forces from the time of his reception into the transit camp, until the time of his departure (this would in fact mean that airmen would be subject to military, not Air Force, law while at Clairwood). However, a Daily Routine Order was issued on January 26 by W/Cdr. Shenton announcing the formation of No. 2 RAF Detachment, with himself in command at Clairwood, and attached to the IFTC for accommodation and rations only. The airmen put on trial, and who comprised the detachment, were thus made subject to the Air Force Act. Fiddament assumed that the Army authorities agreed to this procedure "on the spot". The War Office certainly had a copy of the Air Ministry signal proposing this procedure and did not raise objections. Therefore, argued Fiddament, the formation of No. 2 Detachment fell outside the scope of the directions in AMO A.1086/41. He thought it advisable, nonetheless, to obtain confirmation from the War Office. Additionally, the authority of the Air Council for the formation of the unit, as advised by McGeagh, should be ensured. In the fullness of time, those procedural requirements were met.

Another legal problem could have been raised, relating to the location of the incident. That was, did UK military and Air Force law apply in the Union of South Africa? This was a more knotty problem and one which appeared to concern the Army authorities. Or at least this seems to be the inference to be drawn from a ruling in the JAG's "Rulings Book" for February 25 1942.[17] The issue explored by the JAG was the scope of the disciplinary powers of the commandant at Clairwood, Col. Stewart, over members of the Imperial Forces in the Camp. The JAG's ruling does not specifically cite the *City of Canterbury* incident by name, and arguably it might have related more generally to allegations of indiscipline or misconduct by British troops billeted at Clairwood. But the broad question of jurisdiction as between South African and UK military law was certainly raised, and the date of the enquiry and legal ruling is surely more than coincidental. The (British Army) Adjutant-General, on behalf of the commandant at Clairwood, had addressed a number of enquiries to the JAG. First, he desired confirmation that the Army Act was applicable to British troops serving in South Africa. In reply, the JAG informed him that this was so, as long as an appropriate Order in Council had been made under Section 3 of the Allied Forces Act 1940. Another route to the same result was via the application of South African legislation, which permitted the service courts of visiting forces to function where the visiting force was present with the consent of the Union government. This was of course a matter of interpretation of South African law, but MacGeagh thought that jurisdiction had thus been transferred to the UK Army Act. The Air Ministry, he pointed out, had been advised in a similar fashion a month previously, when the question of jurisdiction arose in the cases of Poles, Free French and Norwegians being trained in RAF Transferred Schools in Canada.

All the legal difficulties in respect to jurisdiction having been surmounted, the next issues concerned the type of court-martial to convene and the charges to be levied against the accused. On the first question the Air Ministry had already signalled to Pretoria on January 17 that the courts-martial should be field general courts-martial (FGCM), assembled by an officer of not lesser rank than squadron-leader and who possessed a warrant to convene. This latter requirement was strictly speaking unnecessary, though Shenton, the convening officer, did possess such an authority. As the *Manual of Military Law* made clear,[18] an FGCM had the same jurisdiction as a general court-martial, including the power of trying an officer, but it was convened in an exceptional way, in that the convening officer required no royal warrant before assembling the court-martial. The FGCM was also subject to exceptional rules whereby the procedure was of a more summary character than a general court-martial.

Basically this meant that the statement of the offence might be made briefly in any language sufficient to describe or disclose an offence under the Army or Air Force Act. It also meant that an FGCM could, if military exigencies or other circumstances dictated, dispense with the elaborate form-keeping associated with the conduct of courts-martial, except that such written record as seemed practicable should be kept by the provost-marshal or APM, if present; or, if not, by the president and officer charged with promulgating the finding. This written record was to correspond as accurately as possible to the contents of the requisite forms, stating at least the name or description of the accused, the offence charged, the finding, sentence, confirmation, and any recommendation to mercy. The military exigencies or other circumstances had to be explained to a superior authority in order to justify the departure from strict procedure.

An FGCM could only be convened on active service or abroad for the trial of offences which it was not practicable, "with due regard to the public service" (which often meant speed), to try by an ordinary GCM. The FGCM had to consist of not less than three officers, unless the convening officer believed that three were not available; in which case two officers sufficed. In the latter case, the court-martial could not award any sentence exceeding two years imprisonment. Additionally, a sentence of death required the concurrence of all the members of the court. This last point was certainly not wholly irrelevant to the *City of Canterbury* incident. The first batch of accused had been charged with mutiny. As Fiddament minuted to the AMP, "the experience of standing trial on a charge which rendered them liable to the death penalty – this was stressed at the trial – is one they are not likely to forget."[19]

Having thus decided upon an FGCM, it was left to Shurlock to determine the appropriate charges. He was aware that considerable difficulties had arisen in collecting evidence, in that witnesses were reluctant to testify (many had, of course, sailed away on the ship), and that evidence of identification had proved difficult. Nonetheless, he placed reliance on the initial version of events given by S/Ldr. Erksine, the RAF Embarkation Officer at Durban, according to whom a collective defiance of his order to board the vessel had taken place. We shall explore this claim when the mutineers' own story is told. Meanwhile it may be noted that Erskine's initial account persuaded Shurlock to lay a charge against all the men of "joining in a mutiny", contrary to Section 7(3) of the Army Act and the Air Force Act.

Mutiny in Section 7 implies, according to the *Manual of Military Law* (1914), collective insubordination, or a combination of two or more persons to resist or to induce others to resist lawful military or Air Force authority. A serviceman could not be charged generally with mutiny or with an act of mutiny, but only with some one or more of the specific offences laid down in Section 7. In the *City of Canterbury* incident, the specific offence in Section 7(3) was where a serviceman:

> Joins in, or being present, does not use his best endeavours to suppress, any mutiny or sedition in any forces belonging to His Majesty's regular, reserve, or auxiliary forces, or Navy.

On conviction, the guilty party would be liable to suffer death or such lesser punishment as laid down by the Acts. The notes to Section

Mutiny or Protest?

7(3) in the *Manual* point out that doubts could arise whether men present when a mutiny was being contrived or had actively begun were actually joining in or not. But Subsection (3) appears to suggest that any serviceman not using the "utmost endeavours" which he might be reasonably and fairly expected to employ, in order to suppress the mutiny, would be equally guilty with those actively joining in the mutiny.

Shurlock accordingly advised that the men be so charged and that the courts-martial should proceed in batches of 30 at Clairwood, commencing on January 26. Wing Commander L.M. Hooper, probably with one of the Air Schools in the Union, was appointed to preside over the proceedings. Things did not go according to plan, for in the course of the hearings, which lasted till February 4, the evidence of S/Ldr. Erskine, to the effect that an order to embark had been issued and collectively disobeyed, was rejected. Indeed, before the conclusion of the hearing, Durban RAF Pool signalled to the Air Ministry, complaining that:

> Whole matter most unsatisfactorily handled. Principal witnesses sailed in ship and conviction doubtful in case RAF. Evidence against Army stronger but consider would create friction if conviction in one service but not other as circumstances materially identical. In the event of finding not guilty at first trial, propose abandon trial remainder. Do you agree? In the event of finding guilty may I authorise that court accept plea guilty in respect remainder? . . . understand troops must be available proceed early date. In the event of trial still in progress instruct what action shall be taken. Am opinion troops should proceed next draft as case not strong and evidence discloses considerable mitigating circumstances.

The reply from London a day later was that if the trial of the first 30 RAF men proved abortive, there would be no objection to the withdrawal of the charges against the remaining RAF and Army personnel. If any were to be found guilty, then it was for the discretion of the Durban RAF Pool to decide whether the trial of any or of all the remainder should proceed. The War Office apparently concurred in these views. Finally Durban was reminded by the Judge Advocate General that a plea of guilty could not be accepted if further mutiny charges were laid.

The pessimism reflected in this message was duly mirrored in the outcome of the first court-martial. On its termination on February 4, the 30 airmen were acquitted of the charge of mutiny, leaving a further 130 airmen and 28 soldiers to be tried.

The trial of the Army personnel, one sergeant and 27 ORs, was held next, commencing on February 6.[20] In view of the outcome of the previous trial, Shurlock now advised that in addition to the mutiny charge under Section 7(3) of the Army Act 1881, the soldiers should also be charged under Section 40 of being absent from their place of duty. In this case the NCO was found guilty of joining in a mutiny and sentenced to two years' imprisonment with hard labour, while the ORs were sentenced to 18 months with hard labour.[21]

The more difficult question now arose of what to do with the remaining airmen in view of the acquittal of the first 30 RAF personnel and of the conviction of the soldiers. Eventually Shurlock decided that, "in the interests of discipline and to prevent what may have been apparent unfairness between the Air Force and the military", he advised that the trial should proceed. He did, however, advise that *only* the Section 40 charge in the Air Force Act, being absent from one's place of duty, should be levied. Presumably the element of *collective* insubordination, necessary to establish the charge of mutiny, was thought by Shurlock to be in some considerable doubt (the account of some of the mutineers would seem to support him).[22]

To save time he arranged for the remaining 130 airmen (less the medically unfit serviceman) to be tried in one batch. As the defending officer indicated that he wished a differently composed court from the one which had tried the first 30 airmen, Shurlock was now required to resolve a further jurisdictional problem. Since all available Air Force officers in South Africa were technically attached to the Union Defence Forces, he had to arrange for the appointee to the court-martial to be detached from the South African Military Discipline Code and become attached to the Imperial RAF Pool at Durban. This was done and the court assembled on February 9, sitting till February 14. All the accused were found guilty and sentenced to one year's imprisonment with hard labour, the NCOs, in addition, being reduced to the ranks. Three different hearings with three different outcomes arising from the same incident was undoubtedly an anomalous outcome. It prompted the JAG to minute to the AMP on May 4 that:

Mutiny or Protest?

it seems to me most unfortunate, and due to the way the cases were handled, that of the 160 [RAF] men who were involved in the disturbance at Durban, 30 have escaped punishment, although obviously equally guilty as those who have now been sentenced to imprisonment.[23]

The prison sentences of all those convicted, with one exception, were suspended, reflecting the wishes of the Air Ministry expressed earlier. The exception related to the Army sergeant, considered by the military authorities to be the "worst offender". The familiar justification for harsh treatment in his case was that the authorities had to demonstrate, through inflicting immediate punishment, the seriousness of the episode.

> Further, our view was that matters of this kind rarely arise without a leader. If it were known in any case that leaders were punished expeditiously, it would have a deterrent effect on producing other leaders.[24]

The sergeant himself had decided to petition the confirming officer against his conviction. Petitioning is a safeguard additional to the reviewing and confirming procedures, to prevent wrongful convictions by a court of military or Air Force officers who are not themselves trained lawyers. Though conclusive evidence is lacking, as all records of individual courts-martial are subject to 75-year closure, it seems that the petition was rejected, after the advice of the JAG had been taken. On the other hand, it is believed that the Army sergeant's sentence of imprisonment, once confirmed, was also suspended, in line with those meted out to the other convicted servicemen,[25] but that he, unlike the others, was returned to the U.K.[26]

Once all the courts-martial had been concluded, the sentences in the case of those convicted were promulgated in parade. The men were subsequently transported back to Durban's Point Docks where most boarded the *Strathnaver* sailing in convoy WS 15 for Bombay. Singapore fell on February 15, the day after the last court-martial hearing finished. As the convoy left South Africa on February 16, two days behind schedule, Shurlock reported that the men, "all sailed as instructed. I personally saw them go aboard".

Chapter 4

The Servicemen's Story

It is a trite comment that history tends to be written by the winning side and that "winners" is an elastic concept which covers not just the victors in battle but the "respectable" elements in society. The views of the "authorities", whether kings, governments, institutions or lawyers, tend to be more accessible for wider historical dissemination than are the views of the common people or the "less respectable" elements. The account of the *City of Canterbury* incident recounted in the previous chapter is the account presented by the authorities (notwithstanding divisions of opinion among segments within authority). For the most part, but not exclusively, it is also a second-hand narrative. It describes events involving *others*, some time after the event; for example, Shurlock's report of the incident to the JAG. It is not the account of the protesters themselves, but interprets the protesters' actions subjectively.

That does not make Shurlock's account any less "correct" than that of the servicemen themselves. It makes it *different*, the explanation for which difference itself being a matter of interpretation. Was he an authoritarian personality and did he consequently wish to emphasise the gravity of their offence by expressing strong criticism of their actions? How did Shurlock's attitude to the men differ from Air Commodore Frew's? Did the latter consider they were more sinned against than sinning? Differences of emphasis among the authorities can certainly be detected in their reconstruction of the events. But their recreation tends commonly to look at events from the top downwards and even if, as with Frew, there is a laudable effort to empathise with the situation of the servicemen, we cannot be certain that their own beliefs are properly understood. For that, we have to ask the servicemen themselves in a neutral environment, where there is no pressure to provide an answer acceptable to the questioner, such as might exist during a court-martial hearing when a defending officer is probing the accused. Ideally such an occasion would be immediately after the event in question, where the investigator can record instantly the feelings and views of his respondents. Nearly fifty years after the *City of Canterbury* incident, we have to make do with a somewhat unsatisfactory substitute. With the exception of those mutineers who kept a daily diary of events, a reconstruction of the incident and the court-martial through the eyes of the protesters, as expressed to the author in correspondence and in interviews, provides an insight which the official version cannot match both in drama and in subjective meaning to the men themselves. It was *their* protest (whether or not they formed the group who remained on the quayside to be driven away to Clairwood and court-martial once the ship had sailed). It is *their* account which is presented here.

Members of all three services in the British armed forces boarded the ship at Point Docks, Durban, on January 12 1942. There were naval ratings, 80 according to A.P. Wheway, who was F/Sgt. (Clerical) with the ship's service staff at the time. They were awaiting dispersal on ships in the Far East and included some Royal Marines, maybe 30 to 40. There was an Army company of under 400 men, No. 4 Ordnance Store Company, RAOC, destined for Singapore and under 1,000 RAF personnel. Most of the airmen were skilled ground crew who were to be sent to those airfields in Malaya still left in British hands. Finally about twenty Australian, British and Canadian sergeant-pilots, under the command of a wing commander, were also being sent out on board the *City of Canterbury* to fly planes in a desperate bid to stop the Japanese advance.[1]

Among the naval draft was twenty-year-old Joe Morrison, now of Grangemouth, who was an engine room artificer (ERA). Like many of the *City of Canterbury* draft, he had transferred from the *Athlone Castle* where he had enjoyed a cabin and all meals served to him. The new conditions were primitive by comparison. Another member of the mixed naval party, which probably included stokers and ABs for onward drafting once they had arrived at their destination, was William Kinnear of Glasgow, due to join HMS *Danae* as ship's butcher. His party, who were first aboard the *City of Canterbury*, had found her filthy and smelly and had started cleaning up and disinfecting the messes. When the Army and RAF contingent went

The Servicemen's Story

aboard, and when most of them promptly walked off again, the authorities responded by cancelling shore leave for the remaining servicemen on board. On the morning of the day when the ship was due to depart, Kinnear and a companion managed to sneak ashore to keep a date, by concocting a fictitious letter to be delivered to the Naval Commander at Tribune House, Durban. When they returned hours later, the ship was already miles away and steaming for the Far East.

Not only AWOL, they could now even be classed as deserters, especially as they chose to travel to Johannesburg for about nine days before giving themselves up to the military authorities. Summary disciplinary steps were taken against them, resulting in 42 days in Durban civil jail, a mercifully light sentence, in William Kinnear's judgment. He was then ordered to fulfil his postings to the *Danae*, but he never quite caught up with her, as a succession of postings on other ships, including HMS *Maidstone*, a submarine depot ship at Mombasa, took precedence. Strictly speaking the twenty-six-year-old William Kinnear was not part of the protest movement which led to the courts-martial of the 188 Army and RAF personnel. He was merely conducting his own private resistance to authority.

The main Army contingent, No. 4 OSC, had departed from Avonmouth on the *Highland Princess* and sailed north to join the rest of the convoy at Gourock. On their eventual arrival at Durban, they spent a few days on the *Andes* before being trans-shipped to the *City of Canterbury*. Pte. Evans' diary entry, offering an unflattering view of the ship as, "7,000 tons of dirt and rust which had just brought a load of Italian prisoners from the Western Desert", was somewhat mild. More vociferous criticisms reached the ear of the OC No. 4 OSC, Major Robert Peaty, whose own cabin, he soon discovered, was infested with insects. He authorised a small deputation of his warrant officers and senior NCOs to see Captain Percival. Selected by his senior WO, Sergeant-Major True, they included Sub-Conductor [i.e. WO2] Ron Hastain, a Fleet Street journalist in civilian life. Captain Percival, the master of the *City of Canterbury*, gave the impression of being unaware of the conditions on board, but a cleaning operation was agreed. Both Staff-Sergeant Doug Hanson and the late Pay Sergeant Ron Clayton later recalled the protests and remembered setting about cleaning their quarters, suitably armed with disinfectants and insecticides.

Durban 1942: A British Troopship Revolt

This additional application of elbow-grease failed to satisfy large numbers of the men on board. For, in addition to the RAF ground crews who left the ship, many men from No. 4 OSC, including a lance-sergeant, walked off. As we already know, 27 soldiers and one sergeant were left behind as the ship sailed. We shall come back to No. 4 OSC in due course.

The RAF personnel constituted by far the largest contingent on board the ship. The vast majority were, as already indicated, ground crew personnel, most of whom had probably been engineers, shipbuilders, joiners or electricians prior to enlisting. Joe Fishwick from Peterlee was a "chippy rigger" (joiner), David Sharp of Greenock was a fitter/armourer (torpedoes), Jim McGeorge of Edinburgh was a radar operator. Some, like John Nevin, a "General Duties" man from West Yorkshire, would describe themselves as a "Jack-of-all Trades, Master of None", while William Batchelor of Crieff was an M.T. driver.

The uncleanliness of the ship was the most obvious feature to strike those who boarded the *City of Canterbury* after the comfort of the *Andes* and the *Athlone Castle*, and after the superb hospitality of Durban and her residents, but there were other causes for complaint. Though Mr. G. Walmsley of Accrington and the late Ron Farringdon of Bedford found the food satisfactory, David Sharp recalls that for two days at Durban, the draft received no hot food and no fresh food. Everything was out of tins. Perhaps it was reasoned that on shore leave all the troops could enjoy the exotic fruits available in abundance. The provision of cold food at least would have been some comfort to Hugh Preston, assigned to galley fatigues while the ship was docked at Durban. Ron Farringdon recalled in his diary that, for eating purposes, each serviceman was allocated a seat at a table. Two orderlies from each table had to go to the galley to collect the food and then serve it up. Even were it not for the dreadful condition of the accommodation left after the Italian POWs had disembarked (whom rumour had it would be sent to the UK on the *Athlone Castle*, a rumour tailor-made to increase the anger of the servicemen aboard the *City of Canterbury*), what was made available to the men was considered pretty grim. They were expected to eat and sleep in the cargo holds, adapted as mess decks only by the expedient of slinging hammocks ("beastly things", according to Ron Farringdon) above tables and not everyone was successful in obtaining a hammock. Even those lucky enough to obtain hammocks were not persuaded of their good fortune. Terence Billing of Norwich, for example, one of those court-martialled, recalls unrolling his hammock and finding it crawling with bed bugs. Venturing into the galley with some mates, he saw a continuous army of cockroaches marching across slabs of butter placed on shelves. Apart from the insects a major discomfort was the intense heat below decks. Edwin Knight of Winchester recalls that there was no fresh circulating air, only a wind scoop which did not work effectively. Edward McDaniel from New Eltham, London, also notes that many of the draft looked for sleeping space on the outer decks, a risky business as rainstorms were quite common. Some RAF sergeants appeared on the mess deck but did not stay long. Walter Adam, a Scot now living in Sutton Coldfield, soon found space with about six other NCOs next to the ship's office.

We have thus delineated as clearly as possible the events leading up to the protest walk-off by the servicemen. We have seen how cramped, how uncomfortable and especially how unpleasant were the conditions, and have observed how sharply they contrasted with those aboard the ships which brought the men from the UK. The relative deprivation of the men, the comforts available in Durban, their inexperience and youth (in most cases) were all relevant. Destination Singapore seems, in general, not to have been a factor. Many of those who sailed on the *City of Canterbury* from Durban did not in fact know for certain where they were heading until much later during the voyage. When the protesters were addressed by senior officers on the quayside to board the vessel, they were only told in general terms of the plight of their fellow-servicemen in the Far East whom they were going to help out. Leading Aircraftman Fred Welding was better informed, however. In his war narrative, he commented:

> I must say that there was an added incentive [for leaving the ship], as in watching the loading of big boxes onto the ship, I had observed the words SINGAPORE stencilled on the cases. I had read the daily papers in Durban and had seen a map showing the steady advance of the Japanese down to Singapore, and it struck me as a not too desirable place to be going to.

Durban 1942: A British Troopship Revolt

Yet it is fair to say that this view was not shared by most of those who walked off the ship. David Sharp, who had been specifically posted to Singapore, claims that the officers were told that the men were quite prepared to go to Singapore, but not aboard the *City of Canterbury*. What then triggered the mutiny? That is, what transformed the grumbling into the overt action of a refusal to tolerate the conditions, leading to the failure to board the ship before she sailed? A number of different accounts, sometimes conflicting, are available, but the germ of the idea of a mass walk-off seems to have originated from among the sergeant-pilots aboard the ship, with the Australians being prominent in the agitation.[2] According to Ron Carter of Sheffield, then a nineteen-year-old aero fitter II, these pilots had been discussing the conditions aboard the ship with servicemen returning to the quayside around midnight, when their shore leave of January 12 ran out. More and more servicemen were turning up, some being driven to the dock by their Durban hosts for that day. On their arrival, remembers J.C. Smith of Cardiff, they were asked which ship they were from. All those from the *City of Canterbury* were told that no-one was going aboard her because of her condition, while others were persuaded to leave the ship to attend the protest meeting. Doug Hanson recalls that, of his army unit, about 30 men joined those at the meeting outside the dock gates. The mood of the men was one of anger, and confusion in the dock area was marked. Some officers appeared on the scene, including the Sea Transport Officer who, according to Jim McGeorge, told the men to get aboard, a demand which provoked a lot of backchat and booing. One warrant officer, swearing at the men and distinctly the worse for drink according to Ron Carter, made matters worse by firing his revolver at the group, fortunately missing. It was all that was needed to turn a milling crowd of complainants into a coherent group defying authority. An armed sergeant-pilot grabbed the warrant officer as other pilots drew their revolvers. Ron Carter thought a gun battle was about to break out, but the pilots calmed down and disarmed the warrant officer. He was ordered on to the ship under arrest by a squadron leader. A different version of the discharge of the revolver exists, however. According to Ron Farringdon, a number of military policemen arrived on the scene and an "immigration" officer (perhaps S/Ldr Erskine, the *Embarkation Officer*, who arrived at 0225 hours, or Major Clarke, D/AQMG, who arrived about half-an-hour earlier) addressed the men. He said their comrades were fighting the Japs and badly needed their help, and in spite of the poor conditions on the ship, they should go aboard. To make this point, Ron Farringdon explained, the officer fired his revolver into the air.

Terence Billing's recollection was that his W/Cdr. CO came down from the ship with some fellow officers, and ordered the protesters back on board. Given a rough reception, he grabbed an airman and threatened to shoot him if his order was not obeyed. As nobody moved, he pulled out his revolver and pulled the trigger. A loud bang was heard and the airman fell down. But the shock was mainly felt by the CO. For he had loaded his revolver with blanks and presumably feared that a live bullet had been accidentally inserted. The airman recovered.

For the next couple of hours arguments and shouting continued to take place, then groups of servicemen began to disperse in all directions. Some of those aboard other vessels tied up at the quayside, one of which was the *Ile de France*, also joined the crowds on the jetties. Suddenly an armed party of soldiers (whether they were military policemen is not confirmed) drew up in trucks and took up stations. They attempted to round up the protesters but the servicemen had scattered in all directions. Eventually the armed party placed a guard on the dock gates, only allowing through those who would board the ship. A naval officer, presumably from the STO division, warned those still refusing to board that they had a very short time to change their minds, after which, if still maintaining their protest, they would be arrested. As well as this threat, there was in fact also issued, according to Edwin Knight, a promise made by the OC Troops, W/Cdr. Kercher, that if the men went on board, something would be done in the morning to deal with the complaints. The number of protesters still holding out at 2.30 in the morning was dropping fast. "As the crowd grew less", wrote Ron Carter in his diary, "all had the same thought, that as soon as only a few remained ashore, they'd be grabbed as ring-leaders; so consequently . . . all went down-heartedly aboard". The ship was moved a few feet from the jetty and the gangway pulled up. The night escapade was over.

A night of "intense misery" (in the opinion of Ron Carter) was then endured by the men trying to grab some shut-eye in the mess decks.

Durban 1942: A British Troopship Revolt

But, "bitten alive and feeling filthy", and surrounded by grime and grease on the tables, some of those who could not obtain hammocks tried to sleep on the floor. Many others sat back to back on benches on each side of the tables. Some sat up all night smoking. Toilet and washing facilities were woefully inadequate for the 800 or so crammed into that particular mess deck. The condition of the life-jackets and belts and indications of rotting timber in the life rafts added nothing to the security and comfort of the men.

At last morning broke and a breakfast comprising bread and tinned salmon was provided. The events of the night before had only postponed a more serious confrontation. Aircraftman Edwin Knight concluded that the authorities' plan was to get the ship away from the docks as quickly as possible to prevent more trouble erupting. Armed guards were put on the gangway with orders to stop anyone from going ashore. But moves were already afoot among the men on board to renew their protest by a mass walk-off, perhaps triggered by an insistence on going down the gangplank to buy fruit from sellers near the quayside. It is possible that different groups of servicemen aboard the ship were thinking and planning the same thing. LAC Fishwick and his mates had spent the night lying on a grill which slotted across one of the holds. The smell from the vegetables in the hold below was overpowering. They organised a delegation to ask the CO what was happening, but were told merely to be prepared to leave.

They did leave but down the gangplank, down the berthing ropes and even jumping off. LAC Welding was approached by a "little fairhaired corporal", who said they ought to protest about the conditions and that the way to do it was to walk off the ship and to refuse to sail except in another vessel. Welding thought about it for a moment, recalling his schooldays when a protest walk-out from detention fizzled out because most of the boys, including the one who had suggested the idea, failed to take the crucial steps. This deterred him, but when he saw that a large number of his fellow-servicemen were in fact leaving the ship, he decided that, "I might just as well go, as it was going to be a full blown walk-off". David Sharp took part in a meeting of some of the men, "unknown to anyone, and made up our minds what we were going to do", that is, to stage a walk-off. AC2 Hugh Preston left the ship at 10.30 a.m., while Cpl. Lenzi of No. 4 OSC, curious to know what was happening

The Servicemen's Story

on the quayside, went down the gangplank, past the armed guard, with Pte. Pressley.

The sergeant-pilots, who had been instrumental in the previous night's disturbance, meanwhile renewed *their* protest and asked for the support of other RAF men in walking off the ship and demanding that it be fumigated. Ron Carter remembers that, "the lot did [walk off], knowing unity is strength". Although the troopship sergeant-major told the protesters that the ship's crew were doing their best to remedy matters, and that plenty of cleaning materials had now arrived, the walk-off was well under way by then. A few of the men had tossed their kit-bags onto the dockside, had jumped off the ship or had simply gone down the gangplank, and, recalls Jim McGeorge, encouraged everyone else to join them.

How did they get past the armed sentry on the gangplank? According to Eddie Knight, the sentry jabbed with his bayonet at one man coming down from the ship and that was the spark which set the tense situation alight. A rush was made for the gangplank and the men streamed down. Ron Carter recalls that, at that point, no-one stopped the men (how could they?), and that even the sergeant in charge of the guard on the gangplank did not seem to mind. He and his guards reportedly soon joined the protest. Edward McDaniel recalls a wing-commander (Kercher?) reducing the sentry to tears by ordering him to shoot the first man coming down, while David Sharp remembers that when an officer (presumably the same one) ordered the guard to start shooting, he refused, gave the rifle to the officer and told *him* to fire if that was what he wanted. The officer declined the offer.

The arrival of Air Commodore Frew on the scene put a different complexion on the affair. He was shown over the ship by a delegation of the men, and agreed that the vessel should be fumigated before sailing. He apparently disappeared for some time and then returned with the news that as the ship was due to sail at 2.30 p.m. (it was already lunch-time), the cleaning would not be undertaken before then, but that there might be a replacement ship at Mombasa. The men on the quayside were told that the draft were bound for Singapore with badly needed equipment (in fact, many of those who sailed from Durban were unsure of the destination till much later). Frew also told them that their fellow-countrymen already there were in great danger and needed their support. Those still on the dockside should go on board or take the consequences, whatever they might be. Further exhortations were also made. As LAC Welding wrote in his war narrative, "a junior officer came ashore, got up on a packing case, and appealed to us as good loyal British citizens and fighters for freedom to go back on board". He was probably a lieutenant with No. 4 OSC, so wrapped up in his pleas that he himself almost "missed the boat". The sergeant-pilots, having been promised accommodation on deck (it had been rumoured they had been offered officers' quarters, but in fact, they were told to sling hammocks between the derricks), agreed to climb on board, leaving the RAF and Army personnel on the dockside, until a trickle of disconsolate British servicemen began to join them on the ship. Gradually this trickle increased, until the vast majority were back on board. Captain Percival then announced that the ship would be departing in 30 minutes and though shore leave had been cancelled, it is not clear that any announcement over the tannoy had previously been made that the ship was under "Sailing Orders" (otherwise, William Kinnear would not have risked going ashore).

Central to this description of events is that no *orders* to go back on board ship were given to the men, an interpretation which the subsequent courts-martial accepted and which, as already explained, prompted W/Cdr. Shurlock, the DJAG, to drop the mutiny charge. Although the evidence of the RAF Embarkation Officer, S/Ldr. Erskine, to the effect that he *did* order the men back on board, was discredited by the conflicting evidence presented to the court-martial, some of the testimony available to the present author suggests that confusion over this critical issue was understandable. Edwin Knight, who was not one of those who remained behind, noted that after Air Commodore Frew had asked the men to *please* return on board and had then left the scene, a naval officer (possibly a lieutenant commander) addressed the men: "You have your orders, now get on board". He was quickly reminded that the men were asked, not ordered, to board her. "I am ordering you", he replied. Then according to Knight, the "Mutiny Act" was read (according to RAF Sergeant Walter Adam, the Riot Act was read out). Doryn Pote's "quiet and polite young RAF man" told her that the officers harangued the men, and threatened them with charges of desertion. Gradually the bulk of them clambered back. "If we had been a group of Australians", he complained, "they would never have talked anybody back on board", an ironic statement given the actions of the Australian sergeant-pilots in abandoning the British servicemen to their fate.

Joe Fishwick remembers the CO coming down the gangplank with other officers and then telling (i.e. ordering) the men to return to the ship, as she was about to sail. "No-one moved. Then the CO walked among us and suddenly he grabbed me and as much as said I was the ringleader, and I hadn't said a thing." Joe's mate from Alva, Clackmannanshire, knocked the officer's hands off him and pulled Joe away into the crowd. The two ORs concluded that the officers were only looking for a scapegoat.

These accounts certainly give the impression that an order to board the vessel *was* given, though none of the accounts nearly 50 years after the event unequivocally confirm S/Ldr. Erskine's story. His statement of evidence to the court-martial recounted:

> At 10.30 hours on 13/1/42, I attended an inspection of the ship with the Senior Transport Officer (i.e. Cdr. Burgess-Watson RN). It was impossible to make a complete inspection of the ship as four to five hundred men had returned to shore. I returned to HMT CITY OF CANTERBURY at 1400 hours and a large number of men who should have been on board were on the dock. I went to the dock and I said to all RAF personnel present, "I am the Embarkation Officer and order you to return to the ship immediately". They defied my order.[3]

S/Ldr. Erskine's M.T. driver, LAC George Watts, confirmed his testimony, and swore that Erskine, "approached these men and addressed them. He [Erskine] said, 'I am the Embarkation Officer. My duty is to order you to return to the ship' ". Of course, it is conceivable that the person (if any) issuing an order to board the ship was one of the officers who actually sailed on the *City of Canterbury*; in which case, he would not have been present at the court-martial to speak to his order. It is, however, beyond dispute that the court refused to accept the veracity of Erskine's evidence and that Shurlock ultimately agreed with this assessment.

Order or no, we have seen that the trickle of men responding to it (or to the request) soon became a large-scale return to the ship. LAC

Durban 1942: A British Troopship Revolt

Welding watched them board the ship but decided to sit tight and see what would happen:

> "The whistle of the steamer was blown a couple of times and a loud hailer was produced on deck and we were told it was our last chance as the boat was sailing immediately. There were about 150 of us still on the dockside and none of us moved. Next minute the gangplanks were up, another whistle from the boat and off she went – admittedly to my surprise as I thought it was a bluff. She disappeared from sight and we stood about wondering what the next move would be".

Ron Carter also thought that the raising of the gangplank at 2.35 p.m. was a bluff, especially since all the men had been warned that the ship would sail at 2.30. Nonetheless, at the raising of the gangplank a number of men, according to S/Ldr. Erskine, started to run back to the ship and tried to board her by means of rope ladders. Some, according to Ron Farrington, "ran and took a flying leap and gripped the side of the boat and were pulled aboard by their comrades". John Nevin, the "Jack-of-all Trades", was one of these. So was the late George Paterson of Liverpool, who also kept a diary of the events. Then the gangway was lowered again for another ten minutes to allow a last opportunity of embarking. Major A.E.N. Clarke of the Imperial Movement Control division at Durban, noted that a further number of RAF men and some soldiers availed themselves of this final opportunity.[4]

But if the view of William Docherty of Glasgow is representative of those who stayed behind, what was the point of going back on board when the ship was still in the same state? At 1451 hours, precisely, the *City of Canterbury* left Point Docks.

The impact of what had occurred had not really sunk in among the 188 servicemen left behind. It was raining hard at the time and many of the men were in fact sheltering or resting in sheds along the dockside. As a result, they did not even see, or know, that the ship was departing. These men, in particular, were reluctant, even accidental, mutineers, and it was galling for them to realise that with the departure of the ship, also went their kit and personal belongings. LAC Welding thought about making for the Embarkation camp, but before a group of them could move off, a number of Army trucks drew up, and an officer, probably with the Witwatersrand Rifles, jumped

The Servicemen's Story

out with a platoon of soldiers carrying rifles with fixed bayonets. The mutineers were told they were under arrest and would now be taken to Clairwood Camp. S/Ldr. Erskine reported that he counted 160 RAF men who were then marched off by Captain Henry Yates of the South African Air Force, who was attached to the RAF Embarkation Office at Durban. According to Welding, the armed soldiers accompanying them seemed highly amused at the incident and a sergeant said, "Don't worry, you blokes. We're not going to shoot you". They marched off through the outer suburbs, with Captain Yates at the head of the column, and they started singing an old service song, "Lulu, that Zulu Girl of Mine". Welding remembered passing a white woman with her two children standing at the gate of their home and looking at the column with a "frankly disapproving" face as the servicemen marched by.

The critical expression on her face testified, perhaps, to the local knowledge of the affair which had percolated through the district. Ron Carter concluded that all Durban now knew of the incident:

> and the cars that came down to the docks were endless. Reporters also came down and got all the "gen" from the boys who were too indignant to withhold anything.

Yet, as he also noted, there was nothing subsequently written about it in the local press. The authorities had managed to suppress wider knowledge of it. "Nevertheless," he felt, "everyone in town knew the whole proceedings, so it didn't matter much, and we had the majority in our favour." The broader repercussions of the affair, in the context of the South African political scene, will be examined later where the censoring of details of the incident will be considered and an explanation offered.

Having reached Cato Street Dock Gate, the party were loaded on four troop carriers at about 4.45 p.m and were then driven off to the camp. In charge of them for the journey was Major H. Stewart, Assistant Camp Commandant, who accompanied Major Cuthbert Steward, Deputy Assistant Provost-Marshal at Durban, in his own vehicle. Finally, the column reached Clairwood at 5.30 p.m., where Pilot Officer R.S. Gordon-Brown, an RAF administrative officer at the camp, had been forewarned to expect their arrival. Cpl. Sidney Reason, from the RAF Orderly Room, accompanied them to No. 3

Durban 1942: A British Troopship Revolt

Lines where they debussed. From there they went to No. 3 Lines Dining Hall, were divided into three groups and a complete nominal roll was taken. They were given a meal (a "wizard dinner", thought Ron Carter), allocated to tents (Ron shared with his two close friends) and then issued with basic kit, which amounted only to blankets, towel, knife, spoon, fork and mug. As for additional items such as razors, tooth brush, comb, shaving brush and hair brush, these had either to be scrounged or paid for, the latter being somewhat difficult as none of the mutineers had any money with them (Fred Welding had only the shirt, shorts and sandals that he stood up in). Indeed, on their arrival at Clairwood, they were instructed that they would be denied service pay except 2s 6d (later increased to 5s) a week, enough, calculated Welding, to buy one cup of tea and a cake each day in the canteen. Still, first impressions of the camp among the mutineers were distinctly favourable. Apart from the high quality of the food, Ron Carter considered the "all-ranks" club was "smashing", the only drawback being the lack of funds with which to enjoy its facilities.

The following morning, after breakfast, the mutineers were paraded before Col. Stewart, the Camp Commandant, who gave them a vigorous dressing-down. "Men of the Royal Air Force," he boomed, "I'm bloody well ashamed of you", recalls David Peacock of Ashford, Kent, who was then an AC2 fitter-armourer. At that stage they were formally told that they were being held under open arrest and confined to camp, a state of affairs whose legality Ron Carter quietly doubted, on the footing that they had not yet been charged with a specific offence. Given the imminence of court-martial proceedings, they agreed among themselves to appoint a spokesman. This was apparently AC1 Smith, D.C.G,. who had claimed some pre-enlistment legal training. Whether that was true or not, Ron Carter felt that he was sufficiently articulate to represent the men's interests, and was diligent in reporting back to his fellow-arrestees. Despite the severe lecture from Col. Stewart, the men were apparently treated fairly by the officers at Clairwood, though David Sharp recalls that the Station Adjutant gave them a hard time. It was said that he did not like the RAF, though there is no evidence as to how he treated the men of the Army unit arrested with the airmen.

For the next month a varied routine of fatigues, roll call (at 0800 hrs, 1400 hrs, 1800 hrs and 2100 hrs), lectures, attendance at the courts-

The Servicemen's Story

martial, and slipping through the hole in the fence to visit Durban or Pingo Beach, occupied the time of the men. Fatigues comprised mainly trench-digging and sandbag filling. Welding assumed that as the "natives" did all the real tasks at the camp, fatigues were allocated simply to give them something to occupy their time. The sandbag filling was not supervised for long, as the corporal in charge got fed up watching them. After one hour he would disappear and would not be seen until the next day.

So after the traumas of the *City of Canterbury*, they were in fact living quite happily at Clairwood, and even had hopes of staying there for the duration of the war. There were apparently a large number of RAF men there who seemed to be permanent fixtures. They were men who had missed their convoy ship for one reason or another (like the mutineers, in fact). According to Welding, some had jumped ship, while others had got drunk and had turned up at the docks too late. One had found a girl-friend in Durban and decided to stay there. None had been prosecuted and they existed simply by staying at the camp and turning up for meals. The absence of pay did not seem to make that much difference. The camp barber was making a useful living by charging 4d per haircut. He had missed his ship over 12 months previously. He was quite convinced that he had been forgotten and was perfectly content with his lot.

Welding was quite shocked by the working conditions the natives had to endure. An immense Afrikaaner would use his long rhino whip liberally to strike any native of whom he disapproved and the natives appeared to accept this treatment with equanimity. That they were only paid 7s 6d a week for their hard toil, Welding considered outrageous. It was not surprising that they would raid the dustbins on camp to extract anything of use, an expedient to which Welding had been driven only once, that is, immediately on his arrival at the camp. His friend, John E——, another of the mutineers, told him of his visit to the home of an English family soon after the arrival of the servicemen at Durban:

> To my surprise, [wrote Welding] he came back to the camp very early. He told me that he sat down to dinner with the people and a native servant came in with a dish of vegetables which he accidentally spilled on the floor. At this, the master of the household leapt up, seized a cane

and started beating the man unmercifully. John protested at this and got up and came out of the house, saying he was not going to stay under these circumstances.

Though Welding reasoned that such behaviour was not general, he was nonetheless aware of how desperate South African blacks must have been to tolerate working for someone like that English householder.

The international flavour of the Camp was remarked upon by Hugh Preston who noted not only the numerous black soldiers, but also Chinese or Burmese servicemen. Up the road there was also an Italian POW camp whose occupants may have been the cause of much of the trouble aboard the *City of Canterbury*.

For social activities camp residents could enjoy draughts, darts, billiards, table-tennis, the cinema or a concert at the YMCA or the Services Club, as well of course as the impromptu concerts in Montgomery Hall and Tedder Hall. There were also illicit pleasures to enjoy, though no doubt of a sort to which the authorities turned a blind eye. The "mutineers" were officially confined to camp, with frequent roll calls, but as High Preston recalled, "some chaps are inclined to spoil things by being late at parade and neglecting duties". One possible reason is that they were enjoying themselves at the beach or in the town, having crawled through the celebrated hole in the fence. A stroll down to the native village adjoining the camp, passing the sugar plantations and reservoir on the way, and being careful to avoid the snakes, was occasionally taken. Both Hugh Preston and Fred Welding took advantage of this opportunity. On another occasion, Fred decided to make for a local seaside resort with a swimming pool, eventually obtaining a lift in a large open limousine driven by a chauffeur with a couple in the back who seemed strangely uncommunicative. He thought they might have been German sympathisers. The man reminded him of Goebbels.

Another mutineer, in respect to whom it will be understandable if discretion dictates anonymity, decided to walk into Durban with his mate after 9 p.m. roll-call. After a short time, they reached a local railway station and boarded a train to a place called Winklespuit, where they alighted. Drawn to the bright lights of a large hotel with sunken garden and dance floor, they sat down at a spare table, declined to order drinks which they could not afford and surveyed the scene. At a nearby table were two South African Army officers with two girls. One officer invited the RAF men to join, an offer gratefully accepted. A bottle of scotch was quickly consumed, the officers got up to dance with the girls and then seemed to disappear. Next, the camp escapees found themselves at the girls' bungalow which looked out to sea. It seemed to be the classic scenario about which the servicemen had been warned by their officers while on board the *Andes*. Afrikaaners, they were told, were quite likely to be sympathetic to the Germans but our young airmen suspected nothing. Until, that is, more whisky was produced and the questioning started. What were the troop movements, which ships were the airmen from, and so on? They were able to deflect the questions subtly without causing offence and appeared to fall asleep following their drinking session.

After breakfast the following morning, the girls, somewhat restrained, drove the servicemen back to Clairwood in a large Cadillac. The airmen, instead of sneaking back through the hole in the fence which they felt might be embarrassing or undignified in the presence of the two girls, summoned up the courage to march, bold as brass, through the main gates of the Camp, awaiting with trepidation the challenge of the guardroom orderlies, demanding where they were returning from at that time. No challenge came. Instead the penniless adventurers were back in time for a second breakfast and for 9 a.m. roll-call. Of course, when they told their fellow-mutineers, "no-one would believe Norman and [me]; as usual we were accused of 'Shooting a Line' ".

At the beginning of February, Hugh Preston wrote that the authorities put under close arrest about 20 soldiers who had broken camp. The poacher now became gamekeeper and Preston found himself on 24-hour duty guarding those prisoners. Conditions in the guard room were poor, sleeping was virtually impossible and the food was bad. "We carried batons; all of it seems a waste of time, just a damned lot of red tape."

Before this there was some serious business to be dealt with at Clairwood; the *raison d'être* for their presence there in fact. On January 21, that is a week after their arrival at the camp, during which time there had been much coming and going between AC1 Smith, on behalf of the men, and the authorities, the arrestees were issued with a charge sheet and a "summary of evidence". The following Monday (January 26) another meeting of the group was held at which the nature of the charge was explained to them "in understandable English", remarked Ron Carter. The charge was, of course, one of taking part in a mutiny on the *City of Canterbury* and of failing to obey orders to return on board. For this they could have been lined up against a wall and shot if found guilty. During the First World War, many servicemen had been court-martialled and shot for less.[5] Apart from the fact that the whole climate of opinion was against executing Allied servicemen for war-related capital offences during the Second World War,[6] the Durban accused now had the benefit of an experienced barrister, F/Lt. L.J. Biddle, rumoured to be a King's Counsel, who had been assigned to the defence and who took over the work which AC1 Smith had begun. Biddle, recalls Ron Carter, told the group that the defence would be a "piece of cake" since all the men had denied hearing any orders to board the ship, as recounted earlier. Nor had they created any violent disturbances which might have been interpreted as co-ordinated, mutinous behaviour. The following afternoon they met Biddle again and were issued with charge sheets and statements of evidence which replaced those distributed the previous day.

> To my mind [Ron Carter felt] the evidence is a pack of lies in places, but that is my mind – one has to prove these things – my opinion is beginning to fade. How things can be twisted around in legal proceedings is now being brought home to me forcibly.

They were told that the courts-martial would commence at 9 a.m. two days later, on Thursday, January 29, and would be conducted in groups of 30 accused. On the 28th a further meeting with Biddle was held in No. 2 Dining Hall. Hugh Preston recalled that there were a lot of conflicting views as to what actually happened on the dockside. But Biddle was a "very good fellow, a civil lawyer in peacetime with a great sense of humour".

At last the court-martial of the first 30 men was held, whether chosen at random or grouped according to age is not wholly clear, though the former seems more likely; they were all acquitted of the charge of mutiny after a hearing lasting from January 29 to February 4. The news that the court had agreed with the defence that no order to board the *City of Canterbury* had been issued, cheered up the rest of the

The Servicemen's Story

RAF men. Fred Welding concluded that, "we would all be set free". But, as he ruefully added, the authorities had another card up their sleeve. The mutiny charge was dropped, and instead, a Section 40 charge was levelled against the 130 remaining airmen. Section 40 Air Force Act was the provision which, explained Welding, "embraced anything from walking about with your hands in your pockets, to striking a superior officer". He feared the worst, especially since a local barrister, he believed, had been selected by the authorities to conduct the next round of prosecutions.[7] Nonetheless, more meetings were held between the airmen and their defending counsel. On February 2 they were asked to draw a sketch of the positions in which they had been standing when S/Ldr. Erskine allegedly gave his order to board the ship. The following day Biddle assured them that they also would be acquitted. On February 5, the day of the arrival of the *City of Canterbury* at Singapore, Biddle informed them that the mutiny charge had been dropped but that a Section 40 charge had been substituted. As the first 30 had been acquitted of everything, they were "going to fight it like hell" (Preston). On the 7th, the news that the Army sergeant had been found guilty after a two-day trial of inciting mutiny and was liable to severe punishment must have been puzzling, in view of the fate of the first batch of airmen. They were very soon to be enlightened, as *their* court-martial was now set down for the 9th.

At 9 o'clock that morning a roll-call was taken and various persons were sworn in. With the exception of the enigmatic and charismatic Smith all the accused pleaded not guilty. Proceedings were conducted slowly, with hearings taking place only in the mornings. The presiding officer, Squadron Leader Hooper, and the other members of the court (two squadron leaders, David Peacock recalls) sat at a long table at one end of the room, while all the accused sat on wooden benches. Those at the back could only pick up a "mumble" coming from the front of the court. It was not surprising that they found the proceedings rather tiresome, enlivened only by the sharpness of F/Lt. Biddle in ramming home a point in favour of the accused and by barbed comments made by some members of the accused under their breath. David Peacock remembers someone whispering, "Surely those clowns don't take this seriously?" One morning LAC Welding decided to give the hearing a miss, as there no longer were roll-calls. Hugh Preston noted that, at one point, he and his colleagues had made a slip by omitting to tell Biddle that they had signed for some small kit. The significance of this is not clear but perhaps relates to Shurlock's criticism of F/Lt. Bradley, one of the Clairwood staff, whom Shurlock had accused of misleading him by wrongly stating that no kit had been issued to the men (this might have indicated that the draft was not from the *City of Canterbury*).

Then on February 10 disaster appeared to strike the accused. Biddle hurt his arm in the afternoon and had to enter hospital. The court-martial hearing was adjourned to allow the new defending officer time to familiarise himself with the issues. It resumed on the 12th at a new venue, the "Morgue", below the main orderly room of the Camp. The new defending officer, in Preston's opinion, was not as impressive as Biddle. On February 14, the day before the surrender of Singapore, the court reached its verdict. Around lunchtime, Fred Welding's friend, John E——, came to find him. He said, "We've had it, Fred. We've been found guilty and given three years hard labour". Welding nearly fell off the bench on which he had been sitting at the news of the sentence. He had not expected the "guilty" verdict. Then John added that the sentence was suspended: as long as they did not get into any more trouble, they would not have to serve it.

Two days later the men were paraded and marched down to the court room where the sentence was formally promulgated to the men. Though it "staggered" Hugh Preston and, according to David Peacock, caused three of his fellow-accused to faint at hearing the news, it was in fact a suspended sentence of *twelve* months with hard labour, not three years as Welding had been told on the 14th. David Sharp recalls that all the airmen asked to serve their sentences but to no avail. Nonetheless, it followed them on every posting, as every new adjutant religiously went through the expected procedure of asking them for an explanation. In those cases for which the evidence exists, the affair does not seem to have prejudiced the men's chances either of promotion in due course, or of obtaining a character of "Very Good" (the highest awarded in the RAF) by the time of their demob, with the possible exception of two cases. It will be recalled that the suspended sentence of imprisonment would only be triggered in the event of a further conviction during the period of the first suspension. There is some evidence that two of convicted draft fell into that category. Fred Welding hints at this. He remembered that:

The Servicemen's Story

there was one man with whom I shared a cabin on the *Athlone Castle* who, while we were on the boat had said to me that when we got back to the first port of call he would desert the ship and go back to England. He was newly married and spent hours writing letters to his wife. I often wondered what he could possibly be saying to her as life was very uneventful on the troopship. Anyway, when we walked off the *City of Canterbury* he was one of the 150 who came off and stayed behind. He made no more about deserting the RAF and stayed on to be court-martialled with us. I decided that he had obviously had a change of mind and that South Africa was a bit too far away to get back to England.

However, when we were paraded to go to India, he was one selected with my batch, he was missing and we went off without him.

I often wondered if he got back, although actually towards the end of the War, I was talking to a Marine section man who had just come over from England and he said there was a fellow . . . who from my description sounded very like the man I knew and he was stationed at Calshot [near Southampton].

His name was Smith, the smooth-talking spokesman of the group. As Ron Carter pointed out, once F/Lt. Biddle arrived, Smith deserted and was never seen again. Leaving aside the exact timing of Smith's surreptitious departure, it appears that the authorities *did* very soon catch up with him again (as indeed is implied in Welding's narrative). For a cypher message from Lord Harlech to the Dominions Office dated July 10 1942 stated that, together with one other Durban "graduate", AC1 Smith, D.C., after his conviction in February 1942, had *again* been sentenced to eleven months imprisonment with hard labour. The confirming authority recommended that the first sentence be put into execution and that the second one should run concurrently with the first. No doubt to Smith's relief, however, the Air Council had decided that very day, July 10, to remit the sentences on the Durban draft. Whether he ever served time in the glasshouse therefore seems unlikely.

The rest of the draft, after the courts-martial, were allocated to different groups for onward disposal. Hugh Preston, with six or seven close friends, was put on board the troopship *Strathmore* on February 17. She was a three-funneled vessel, more comfortable than the *City of Canterbury* but lacking the luxury of the *Andes*. Still, the overcrowding experienced on his short-lived stay on his previous troopship was mercifully absent. Though he remarked that no other RAF personnel were on board, the *S.A.W.A.S. Book of Thanks* indicates clearly that other airmen, not involved in the Durban affair, were on board her. The voyage to Bombay took over two weeks, the *Strathmore* arriving there around March 4.

The *Strathmore* sailed as part of convoy WS 15, which had arrived at Durban from the UK on February 10. During that first leg of the convoy, the *Llangibby Castle* had been torpedoed about 700 miles off Azores with the loss of 26 men, and had sailed into the town of Horta on one of the islands for repairs to be carried out. The Durban portion of WS 15, code named DM 13, left Point Docks at 11.30 on February 17 under Commodore (Rear Admiral) A.T. Tillard, master of the *Strathnaver*.[8] There were 18 vessels in the convoy and five escorts going to three different destinations, Bombay, Aden and Port T (Addu Attol, at the foot of the Maldive Islands). On February 26 the Bombay section (WS 15B) split off from the Aden section (WS 15A) and comprised just four ships, the *Strathmore*, *Britannic*, *Stirling Castle* and the much slower *Khandalla*, escorted by HMS *Worcestershire*, with Captain W.D. Roach of the *Stirling Castle* assuming the duty of commodore. For those on the *Strathmore* the voyage was uneventful except for an incident on February 19 when a man fell overboard at about 5 a.m; a quick search yielded no result. At 0448 hours on March 4 the Bombay section made rendezvous with the Indian warships, *Lawrence* and *Dipavati*, and was escorted into Bombay at 9 a.m.

Bombay was also the first port of call of Fred Welding once he had sailed from Durban, though it is not clear whether he, too, travelled on the *Strathmore*. Ron Carter's voyage to Bombay was on the *Athlone Castle*, ironically one of the vessels from which some of the airmen had transsshipped to the *City of Canterbury* at Point Docks in January. A number of Ron's close friends sailed with him on the same draft, arriving in Bombay a month after Hugh Preston. Eventually they ended up at the same base, Ambala, which was No. 1 Service Flying Training School, training Indian Air Force pilots. SFTS comprised both an Advanced Training School (ATS) to which Ron Carter was assigned, and an Initial Training School (ITS) where two of his friends were sent. Another colleague of Ron's, Norman K——, was posted to Assam. In early 1943 Ron was sent to Bangalore, where an aircraft factory run by the United States Army Air Force repaired and overhauled Catalina flying boats. Further service saw him with No. 191 Squadron which flew Catalinas and then with No. 240 Squadron, also flying Catalinas. He returned to the UK in October 1945. Hugh Preston spent a few months at Ambala where he met up with some of the *City of Canterbury* airmen, then went to Asanol (West Bengal) in September 1942 and Jessore (East Bengal) three months later.

Another "mutineer", David Sharp, sailed under guard to India aboard the *Strathnaver*, the original commodore ship of convoy WS 15. He recalls that he and his friends had a "rough time" aboard this Army troopship because of the *City of Canterbury* business. The *Strathnaver*, together with most of the ships of WS 15, had been scheduled originally to sail from the UK to the Far East but, as Singapore had fallen two days after the convoy's departure from Durban, their destination was altered. On February 22 *Strathnaver*, escorted by HMS *Ramillies*, left the convoy and made for Port T before proceeding to India.

A number of the mutineers ended up at No. 301 Maintenance Unit at Drigh Road, Sind Desert, Karachi. They included Joe Fishwick and William Docherty. David Peacock, Terence Billing and about four others who also sailed on the *Strathnaver* were sent to No. 146 Fighter Squadron based at Dinjan in Assam. After about a year they were transferred to No. 5 Squadron, arming Mohawks.

In February 1943 Terence Billing was posted to No. 21 Operations Room at Chittagong, staying there, and at nearby Cox's Bazaar, in East Bengal till June 1945. He finished as a corporal at the RAF Delegation in Brussels in 1947. As to the soldiers of No. 4 OSC, including Ptes H—— and W——, the evidence concerning their subsequent destinations is uncorroborated. One view is that around June 1942 they were put aboard the *Orbita* at Durban, whence they were shipped to Liverpool, via Cape Town, where one of them went AWOL before returning to the ship.[9] The army sergeant, another view has it, was sentenced to imprisonment in Winchester Gaol,[10] though whether he served a sentence there, and if so, for how long, is not known. The one destination to where none of the mutineers were sent was Singapore or Batavia.

Chapter 5

Records, Recriminations and Reform

In June 1942, the Director of Personal Services (DPS) at the Air Ministry, Air Vice-Marshal Arthur Fiddament, noted that the 160 RAF men were "probably split up in the Eastern War Zone". He had no information as to their conduct since their courts-martial, nor indeed "whether they are all still alive".[1] Sir Philip Babington, the AMP, in a minute to the Secretary of State, Sir Archibald Sinclair, a month later, thought that the Army personnel had been sent on to the Middle East while the RAF men had been sent "to the Far East where they became involved in the Jap advance".[2] In fact, a South African Air Force communication to the UK Air Ministry in October 1942 confirmed that the airmen had all proceeded to India (eventually including, after his "prior engagement", AC1 Smith, D.C.G., and one other of the Durban airmen whose onward posting had been delayed).[3]

In the normal course of events copies of Form 3104, relating to suspension of sentences, would have been forwarded to the original unit of each of the convicted airmen so that three-monthly reviews of the men's conduct could be undertaken. Wing-Commander Shurlock, the DJAG, did send to the OC Troops on board the ships on which the men were sailing in convoy WS 15 a complete nominal roll of the 190 men involved, together with the information that 157 of them (28 soldiers and 129 airmen), had received suspended prison sentences. This data was to be delivered to the embarkation officer at the men's forward destination. Forms 3104 were meanwhile to be completed by the Air Council, then forwarded to RAF Records Branch in Gloucester, which would in turn send a copy to the new unit of each "convict" in order that the suspended sentence be reviewed periodically. If a serviceman committed another offence, then the sentence of imprisonment would be triggered. As we have already seen, this prospect was one which confronted at least two of the

Durban 1942: A British Troopship Revolt

Durban recalcitrants, AC 1 Smith and LAC F. McK-. What appears to have saved these two airmen from an extended stay in prison was the decision of the Air Council, on July 10 1942, to remit the sentences in the cases of *all* the guilty Durban airmen, although the reduction to the ranks of the sergeant, three corporals and two acting corporals was confirmed.[4] Additionally all the airmen would lose pay for the period in arrest, while awaiting trial. In substance this meant that, although a conviction and sentence of a year's imprisonment with hard labour was recorded against them, they would not have to live on tenterhooks for the next few months in the belief that a conviction for another offence during that period would activate their suspended twelve-month imprisonment. Unfortunately, so far as can be gathered from interviewing some of those convicted, no-one *told* them at the time that the threat of imprisonment for their conduct at Durban had been lifted.

Fiddament observed that this course of action would "not embarrass the Army authorities in any way in their dealings with the soldiers concerned in this trouble".[5] Whereas the remission of the sentences on the RAF men depended on the Secretary of State consenting to the decision of the Air Council, the remission or otherwise of the suspended sentences on the "swaddies" (two years for the NCO and 18 months for the others) depended on their local commander. As the evidence suggests that the Army sergeant was later returned to the UK and his sentence remitted from July 1, it is possible that the sentences on the remaining soldiers sent to the Far East were also remitted.

In the following years, when war service increments were being calculated, confusion remained in some quarters as to whether the airmen's records should contain a note of the suspended sentences. Thus the DPS wrote to the Air Officer in Charge of Records in November 1945, informing him that a number of complaints had been received from airmen involved in the Durban affair, to the effect that their Forms 121 (general conduct sheets) were incomplete inasmuch as no mention was made therein of the suspension of the sentences, though remission from July 1942 had been recorded. The impression was that nearly five months of imprisonment had been served, whereas none in fact had been undergone. Three complainants had been mentioned by name, one of them being Joe Fishwick. The other two were at that time based respectively at No. 24 Air Sea

Records, Recriminations and Reform

Rescue Main Craft Unit and RAF Colerne (near Chippenham). The need was now to scrutinise the other 126 general conduct records, to ensure their accuracy.[6] Even as late as 1951 the AOC No. 18 Group, based at Pitreavie Castle, Dunfermline, was enquiring about the service conduct sheet of Sergeant J.A.—— (an LAC in Durban). He was reassured that the position had now been regularised.[7] Given the original difficulty in identifying the units to which the men belonged, we can scarcely be surprised that information flow was sometimes less than perfect.

In instituting a post-mortem of the incident, the Air Ministry were armed with the damning criticism against the embarkation staff at Durban levelled both by Shurlock and by W/Cdr. Hooper, the president at one of the court-martial hearings. Hooper complained of a "complete lack of initiative" among the RAF embarkation staff in that they had made no effort to induce the servicemen to embark. Secondly, when the recalcitrants were fallen in on the quayside, no nominal roll had been taken, nor had S/Ldr Erskine sought to ensure that the men were "properly cared for" [sic] or charged.[8]

The Sea Transport Officer at Durban also came in for a share of blame, as none of the provisions of King's Regulations, Air Ministry Orders (AMOs) or Army Council Instructions (ACIs), which governed the inspection of troopships, had been carried out. Nor was any excuse for this lapse offered. Hooper recommended that the "embarkation staff be replaced by officers who can be trusted to work without supervision". Finally he noted that only three military policemen had been available to escort the 160 RAF servicemen from the docks and advised that the provost force be increased.

In respect to Shurlock's criticisms, we have already noted his catalogue of complaints. This included the failure of the military and RAF embarkation staff to arrange for the fumigation of the *City of Canterbury*, while she was in the dock between January 7 and 13 (the servicemen had, of course, arrived on the *Andes* and the *Athlone Castle* on January 8); their failure, in breach of King's Regulations, to inspect the ship; the misleading information given him by S/Ldr. Erskine and by F/Lt. Bradley of Clairwood Camp; and the alleged inadequacy of the APM.

Shurlock's hard-hitting report did not please all the senior officers who had to consider it in the aftermath of the affair. The War Office, for example, did not think that his criticism of their Imperial Movement Control officer, Major A.E.N. Clarke, was altogether justified, and he apparently remained in post.[9] Similarly Air Commodore Frew, who had been present at the incident, concluded (perhaps enigmatically) that Shurlock's report "suffers from detachment".[10] If the latter had been on the quayside, thought Frew, he might have modified some of his opinions. In particular, he doubted whether strong measures on the spot, as advocated by Shurlock, would have been effective in quelling the disturbance. In Frew's judgment stronger measures would simply have provoked more trouble, a point of view which Major Peaty clearly held the night before. It had been considered at one stage bringing in an armed guard from among the men still on board the ship, in order to threaten the protesters back to the decks. The idea was rapidly abandoned on the ground that it was unsafe to put firearms into the hands of any of the ship's complement. The sentries on the ship had already, it was felt, demonstrated their unreliability.

Two possible implications can be read into these remarks. The first is that to bring up armed guards on the quayside was to run the risk either that they might side with the protesters or that a wrong move leading to the discharge of a rifle might lead to catastrophic results. The other implication is that the men on the quayside simply needed some gentle, or at least non-aggressive, coaxing to get them back on board. The fact that in the 15-minute period between the scheduled and actual departure times, an "appreciable additional number" of troops returned on board seemed, in Frew's view, to point to the likelihood that a further delay might have seen all the troops back on board the *City of Canterbury*. The evidence from interviews points strongly to the conclusion that the mutineers were merely waiting for someone to take a lead in proposing how to ameliorate the condition of the ship. A promise to fumigate had been extracted but then Frew had reported back that it could not be done. Yet we know from some of those who eventually sailed on her from Durban that a cleaning operation was quickly undertaken once the *City of Canterbury* left port. The indignation and defensiveness of Captain Percival were no doubt an obstacle to sorting out an arrangement which would appease the protesters.

It remains questionable whether stentorian orders to embark would have been heeded without a firm commitment to clean up the ship, let alone whether the "revolt" would have been quickly crushed at the point of a gun, or indeed whether armed guards would have had the stomach to fire.

Frew also added that he considered the criticism of Erskine to be too harsh, given that the job of the embarkation officer at Durban had become extremely difficult. For such an important transit centre the Air Ministry suggested that an officer with experience of home (i.e. UK) embarkations would be appropriate, while an officer with experience of Personnel Despatch Centre (PDC) work should be installed at Clairwood.[11] Frew, while agreeing with these proposals, did not wish his strictures to be read as an adverse report on Erskine.[12]

The Air Ministry approved these proposals in early April 1942 and a month later, S/Ldr. A.L. Redgrove and F/Lt. (Acting S/Ldr.) L.M. Johnston were sent in convoy WS 19 to Durban to assume their new duties as RAF Embarkation Officer and Senior RAF Officer, IFTC, respectively.[13] Erskine was transferred to AHQ Middle East, out of earshot, at least, of the Secretary of State's withering criticism of the embarkation officers and sea transport officer.[14] While the latter was the "most blameworthy" official, the:

> unsuitability of the ship for the transport of troops must have been glaringly evident and, subject to any explanations which the Embarkation Officers may offer, it would seem that their neglect of their plain duty put some hundreds of airmen and soldiers in a very unfair position.[15]

The experience of the courts-martial demonstrated the need to ensure that in any future similar incident, clear evidence should be available to establish:

(a) That personnel disembarked without orders
(b) That they were given a definite order to embark
(c) Identity[16]

In respect to (c) it was apparent that previous trans-shipments of RAF personnel at Durban had not been properly organised, in that drafts and units had not been kept in serials, that officers were not placed in charge of drafts and units, and that unescorted baggage often arrived at the ships from the transit camp. Insofar as each ship leaving the UK had a complete nominal roll of all serials, then there ought to have been no difficulty in preparing new nominal rolls for each trans-shipment (where only part of the convoy from the UK would proceed beyond Durban) and in placing officers in charge of each draft or serial. Yet the trans-shipment details could only be planned locally in the Cape, as the necessary information was not available during embarkation in the UK concerning the capacity and names of ships to be used for the onward journey to the Middle East or India.[17] The Army were to secure two complete ship's staffs to ensure on-the-spot compliance with these arrangements in respect to movements from the Cape to the Middle East, while the RAF was to provide one ship's staff for those voyages where the majority of servicemen were air force personnel.

A review of the RAF Embarkation Office in Durban was attached as Appendix I to the monthly report for July 1942 of Frew's Air Force Mission.[18] Although its authorship is not stated, its contents suggest that it was drafted under S/Ldr. Redgrove's new regime. It addressed itself to the problem of identifying the units and personnel in the drafts being convoyed and recommended implementing the scheme of allocating an officer to each draft, however small. A separate place on board ship should be reserved for each draft where they might parade at different times for disembarkation, having been sorted into nominal roll order. On the ship's arrival, the drafts could be produced and checked rapidly. Re-embarkation problems could be eased by conferring more responsibility on troop deck officers or sergeants prior to the drafts boarding their ship. The previous assumption had been that all re-embarkation duties were the responsibility of the embarkation officer until the servicemen had reached the top of the gangway, at which point his responsibilities for the troops ceased. As the Durban mutineers had all boarded the *City of Canterbury* at least once on January 12 after their trans-shipment from the *Andes* or the *Athlone Castle*, it is possible that S/Ldr. Erskine believed, when the trouble erupted in the early hours of January 13 and again later that day, that it was strictly speaking no longer his responsibility, but that of the troop deck officer or the OC Troops aboard the *City of Canterbury*. This exaggerated division of labour meant that:

Records, Recriminations and Reform

... no Troop Deck Officers or Sergeants were called forward prior to the date of embarkation. If Troop Deck Officers were appointed at all, they were allowed to come forward with the troops on the first trains [from Clairwood] and were merely given instructions to place their hand baggage in their cabins as quickly as possible and proceed to a specified mess deck to take control. In practice they rarely arrived at their appointed Mess Section until after the troops were there, and in any case, knowing nothing of the ships or their duties, they were useless.

New instructions were issued so that troop deck officers and sergeants for each section would be called forward the day before embarkation by the embarkation officer responsible for berthing the ship. The latter would take them round the ship, giving them all necessary information and explaining their duties to them.

This, of course, was all very well if the aim was to smooth the organised transfer of servicemen from one ship to another or from Clairwood to another ship. In the latter case, an elaborate procedure was also worked out to minimise the possibility of servicemen "disappearing" between Clairwood and the Docks; for who knows how many servicemen, enchanted by the idyllic life in Durban, managed deliberately to lose themselves *en route*? If the aim was to grasp the principal issues of the Durban affair, that is ensuring that the ship was habitable and identifying who had ultimate authority over the servicemen in transit, whether the embarkation officer or the OC Troops on board a particular ship, the above outline of the embarkation office's duties was incomplete. The report stressed that the office's relations with Imperial Movement Control, Sea Transport and Union Movement Control were "happy and cordial", and that constant liaison with Imperial Movement Control was maintained regarding the movement of troops. But Shurlock in his report had found fault with all three Imperial units and Frew had also detected deficiencies among these units. The Sea Transport Office, responsible for ship inspection, was, as we have already seen, the subject of comment by Brigadier Falla from the Ministry of War Transport, who recommended that the office be kept separate from that of the (Admiralty) Naval Liaison Office. The War Office, as we have also seen, chose to take no action in relation to Major Clarke of Imperial Movement Control. That left only the question of the division of responsibility for the drafts allotted to a particular troopship. At what point was the embarkation officer relieved of responsibility for the discipline and control of such troops, and when precisely did that responsibility devolve on the OC Troops aboard ship? According to W/Cdr. Shurlock that responsibility remained with the embarkation officer even after the transfer of troops from one ship to another within the port (presumably up to the point at which the receiving troopship left port). Yet though the Air Ministry began to look closely at this question in August 1942, it was, remarkably, November 1945 before a solution was found which satisfied those responsible for drafting the necessary provisions. As time went by more and more complications were discovered; the greater the complexity, the greater the scope for argument.

All we need do here is to indicate broadly the course of debate within the Air Ministry and to note the end result. The opening assumption was that a transfer of responsibility from the embarkation officer to the OC Troops on the *City of Canterbury* would occur once the troops had boarded the troopship. But as Air Vice-Marshal Fiddament's assistant, G.C. Jasper, had minuted to the Director of Movements, Group Captain F.H. Sims, in August 1942:

> If for any reason the ship does not sail immediately and men are allowed to stretch their legs on the quayside, or if the ship calls at an intermediate port and men are allowed ashore, the OC Troops should still be responsible for them although, of course, he may ask for the assistance of the Shore Police. This seems to be the commonsense point of view and the only practicable one.[19]

Given that the embarkation officer would probably have a number of ships with which to deal on the same day, and given that servicemen had been put aboard one ship, the embarkation officer could hardly be expected to have to do the job again some hours later. Jasper ended his note by suggesting that a change to King's Regulations and Air Council Instructions would be advisable. Sims, however, pointed out the provisions in paras. 10 to 16 of Voyage Regulations, which clearly showed that the line of demarcation between the embarkation officer's responsibility and that of OC Troops was literally the ship's rail. Moreover, para. 14 dealt with the question of leave at intermediate ports. In his opinion no clarification of KRs or ACIs was required.

Records, Recriminations and Reform

Jasper persisted by questioning whether the Voyage Regulations *were* as clear as Sims had suggested. Contingencies which involved troops leaving the ship after embarkation were not covered expressly, though he accepted that responsibility remained with the OC Troops by implication. The Voyage Regulations and Instructions for OC Troops had only limited circulation, that is, to ships' personnel and movement control officers. They were not available, "to all who may be concerned such as in this particular incident, where doubt arose in the minds of those who were not immediately concerned with the ship".[20]

Jasper's suggestion that KRs and ACIs be amended to stress the responsibility of the OC Troops until final disembarkation did not actually deal with the situation which had arisen in Durban. As Jasper asked, "were the Durban trouble to be repeated, would the responsibility for getting the men back on board rest with the OC Troops?"[21] It took another two months before Sims replied by claiming that in the event of another Durban incident, it would be the responsibility of the shore officers *and* OC Troops to get the personnel back on board the ship, "not unlike the procedure followed if an airman breaks out of an RAF Station".[22] A direction in those terms would have relieved S/Ldr. Erskine of much of the condemnation heaped upon him for the time when the *City of Canterbury* remained in port.[23]

The department of the Air Ministry responsible for preparing the actual amendments to KRs and ACIs was unhappy about a number of features. Minuting its doubts on December 24 1942, Section 10(a) of the ministry felt that the chain of command ought to be more rigorously defined, especially given the presence at a port of both RAF and Army personnel.[24] Only then could disciplinary changes be considered. In particular it enquired whether, if the OC Troops was an Army officer it was intended that he be entitled to exercise powers, not only of command but also of punishment over RAF personnel, when there was also an RAF officer on board ship (on the *City of Canterbury*, Wing Commander Kercher was obviously senior in rank to Major Peaty). Such a novel departure would require legislative changes. Contrariwise, an Army embarkation commandant then currently held no powers of punishment over RAF personnel, and therefore could not order a court-martial of airmen, no matter whether the offence took place on the quayside or on board the troopship. A final conundrum was whether superior authority for discipline resided with an embarkation commandant whose rank was junior to that of the OC Troops, both officers being in the same service (though it is evident that this did not address the complexity of the Durban situation where S/Ldr. Erskine was junior to W/Cdr. Kercher, but of equivalent rank to Major Peaty).

For nine months these points remained unresolved as the file went missing. Once it was rediscovered, in September 1943, Group Captain Jasper wrote to Sims, informing him that discussions with Section 10 had thrown up further difficulties of inter-service cooperation in respect to disciplinary authority. Jasper once again insisted that a Durban-type situation must be provided for, that is, "when troops disembark at an intermediate port for trans-shipment to another vessel. How is OC Troops then appointed . . .? Should we not make it clear that personnel allowed ashore at any time before sailing (including when at an intermediate port) remain the responsibility of the OC Troops?"[25] We can see that such a provision would have diminished the culpability of S/Ldr. Erskine in the Durban incident, while the beauty of the scheme was undoubtedly its simplicity, even in the confusion of a Durban-style disruption.

Once again, the file went into hibernation or, as G/Cpt. Sims observed on January 10 1945, when it next surfaced, "This file seems to have had an unfortunate career since 24/12/42".[26] As the evidence suggests that his branch were sitting on the file he probably knew this better than anyone. The file was then passed to Section 10 who acidly noted that the Secretary of State's minute of July 1942, demanding that the allocation of responsibility for discipline be clearly settled, had not yet been implemented, "and this would be awkward if another incident of the Durban nature should arise".

After more toing and froing, the problem of securing the appropriate wording of any amendments to KRs, AMOs, ACIs, Army Act and Air Force Act was passed by the DPS (perhaps in helplessness) to the JAG on May 30 1945. Increased urgency now attached to the task since, with the defeat of Germany, "large bodies of troops are being moved about the world in connection with the drafting of troops to the Far East and in connection with repatriation".[27] It was desired, therefore, to avoid any of the jurisdictional problems which had arisen in the

Records, Recriminations and Reform

"serious case of mutiny at Durban" of which Sir Harry MacGeagh, the JAG, was reminded. In response, the Second Military Deputy at the Office of the JAG, W.R.F. Osmond, returned within three days a short draft amendment. This formed the basis of the final Air Ministry version which was eventually issued on October 18 1945, the War Office version, with appropriate wording, appearing on November 9.

Air Ministry Order A. 1026, entitled "Military and Air Forces Acting Together when in Transit at Ports", declared that the OC Troops, of whatever service, was responsible for the command and discipline of all RAF and/or military personnel from the moment they stepped on board the troopship. When ashore in ports, "general control of Army and Air Force personnel was vested in the embarkation commandant, whether a military or Air Force officer, and as long as the ship remained in port, he was also the immediate superior authority of the O.C. Troops" (para. 2). In the Durban incident, it would appear that if this AMO had been in force, W/Cdr. Kercher, the OC Troops on board the *City of Canterbury*, would have been justified in leaving it to S/Ldr. Erskine to exercise his responsibility for discipline over the mutineers. In the event of any disagreement between them as to how to deal with the mutineers, the views of the junior officer, S/Ldr. Erskine, would have prevailed over those of W/Cdr. Kercher. But this interpretation depends on reading the phrase, "from the time they set foot on board", as meaning "during the time they are aboard". For in the case of those who *disembarked* from the *City of Canterbury* in protest, it would have to be assumed that responsibility for their discipline reverted to the embarkation officer, an interpretation in accordance with the provision in para. 2 governing the situation where the servicemen were "ashore in ports".

Suppose, for the purposes of demarcation of responsibility, the phrase, "from the time they set foot on board", is read as meaning that one ignored any subsequent disembarkation of servicemen of the kind which had occurred at Durban, should the OC Troops then remain responsible for the discipline of the men milling about on the quayside or resting on the cotton bales in the sheds at the dockside, even if he were no longer responsible for those who had ventured into the city? Unfortunately AMO A. 1026 failed to clarify this difficult point, by not offering a definitive interpretation of the critical phrase. The order did add that where military and Air Force personnel were acting together either as passengers in transit or as members of the embarkation staff at a port, then the officers and NCOs of one service had the like powers of command and discipline, other than powers of punishment, over the members of the other service. Thus an RAF embarkation officer, for example, would have disciplinary powers over Army personnel who had not yet embarked on a troopship. Again, the Durban difficulty was side-stepped. It was as if the jurisdictional conundra of the *City of Canterbury* affair had never occurred. The impression, in the final analysis, was that, after the event, they had never been grasped.

Chapter 6

The South African Connection

"Elaborate censorship and propaganda is working well and successfully to prevent the truth being known here". Thus wrote Lord Harlech, the UK High Commissioner in South Africa, to the Dominions Secretary, Clement Attlee, in March 1943 about current developments in the Union at that time. His comments were addressed specifically to information on "enemy naval activity . . . sinkings, or anything about ships" within the region.[1] So far as the local South African press were concerned, public knowledge about the Durban troubles a year earlier was just as effectively covered up, though allusions to the events at Point Docks could be faintly detected in the occasional published source. For example, the weekly periodical, the *Forum*, commented in early 1942, in the midst of the Clairwood courts-martial:

> When the censorship blinds are drawn up on this war, no place in the Union will have more secrets to unmask than Durban Bay. There will be tales then of the strange craft that have slipped inside under cover of darkness . . . We may disclose, too, more details of stories of mutinies aboard ships in port here and curious happenings on the quayside.[2]

Censorship during wartime could, of course, be a matter of life and death. The previous month, Rear-Admiral D.A. Budgen RN, Flag Officer in Charge at Simonstown Naval Base, appealed to those living in coastal towns in South Africa to refrain from giving away information of ships' movements:

> If you happen to know that a ship of the Royal Navy or a particularly large convoy or interesting merchant vessel is in port, it requires some self-restraint to refrain from telling your friends and starting an ever-widening ripple of gossip . . . Because you can see a ship lying at anchor from Table Mountain [i.e. Cape Town] or the Bluff at Durban, don't pass

the information on. Do what Nelson did. Turn a blind eye and forget that you've seen it.[3]

The censor did not always show consistency. While the Clairwood courts-martial were securely hidden from the reading public, the court-martial of Captain Maund, the unfortunate captain of the ill-fated *Ark Royal*, torpedoed off Gibraltar in November 1941, was duly reported in the local press.[4]

The difficulties of maintaining secrecy in respect to convoy traffic were well recognised, especially with the major ports playing host to thousands of troops in transit. Thus Captain E.H. Hopkinson, the commanding officer of HMS *Worcestershire* which had been engaged on escorting WS convoys into South Africa, reported to the Admiralty that it seemed to be known ashore in the Union when the convoys were expected and when they were due to sail. He added:

> I am of the opinion that now we are involved in an Asiatic war (the East being the birthplace of intrigue), we must exercise all our imagination and ingenuity to shut down in [sic] leakage of information of value to the enemy.

To this end, "orders, routes, secret charts etc." should be delivered to ships' masters only at the last moment and should be kept locked up until the ship had sailed. "In certain cases, ships sailing until out of sight of land might be instructed to steer courses intended to deceive any observers on land."[5]

The difficulties in South Africa were compounded by the presence of large numbers of Nazi sympathisers among the Afrikaaner population and by the fact that ships would sail up the east coast of Africa past Portuguese Mozambique, an international centre for the kind of intrigue among German, American and British agents (including Malcolm Muggeridge) which Captain Hopkinson associated with the East. Muggeridge, a vice-consul specialising in intelligence work in Lourenço Marques, believed in fact that the Italian consul-general there, Ciampini, "was on the whole more active and dangerous than Wertz", the German representative, and was much surprised when the Foreign Office granted Ciampini a safe conduct to get to Lourenço Marques.[6]

One controversial incident concerned the sinking of the troopship *Orcades* about 250 miles off the South African coast in October

The South African Connection

1942.[7] A German U-boat had successfully planted six torpedoes in her, though evacuation of most of the crew and passengers and their rescue by the SS *Narwik*, a Polish vessel had been achieved. Captain J.C. Annesley, a senior naval officer aboard the vessel, had submitted a report to the C-in-C, South Atlantic, Vice-Admiral C. Tait, indicating his concern that the enemy submarine had not stumbled across the *Orcades* accidentally. Visibility was low at the time of the attack and the chances of a submarine "picking up a ship in the open sea in that weather at that distance from land are so minute that I cannot believe that the meeting was purely coincidental". As an enemy submarine had also been reported to be on the route taken by the *Narwik*, Annesley concluded that leakages of information concerning routes as well as ships were occurring. As the submarine which sank the *Orcades* did not surface, this suggested that the identity of the target had already been known to the submarine captain.

The Director of Naval Intelligence (DNI), on learning of Annesley's report, concluded that two points of importance arose. The first was whether the Naval Control Service Officer (NCSO) in Cape Town was justified in routing the *Orcades* as he did in the light of intelligence about U-boat activities in the area. The second was whether there should be an enquiry into the security of shipping information in South Africa, "as far as the political situation in the Union permits".

With reference to the first point, the evidence showed that the routing instructions for the *Orcades* were known only to the NCSO, Cape Town, and to the ship's master. From that point accounts differed as to what Captain Fox of the *Orcades* was or was not told by Captain May, the NCSO, as to ship sinkings and enemy submarine movements. There was also some confusion about a signal from HMS *Hecla* to *Orcades*, allegedly informing the latter that she was sailing right through a submarine attack track and enquiring who had ordered her to take this hazardous route. According to a signal from the C-in-C to the Admiralty, *Hecla* would be unlikely to have possessed the requisite information to pass on such a warning to the *Orcades*.

Although it was conceded from South Africa that "in the light of after events, it might have been [better] to have held ship", the view was taken that, first, Captain Annesley "produces nothing to substantiate his convictions as regards leakage of information".

Secondly, the possibility of such leakage could not be entirely ruled out, but the number of persons with access to the route was very small, while the security aspect of the NCSO's organisation was kept constantly under review. Thirdly, and more prosaically, the fact that the submarine was in a position to torpedo the *Orcades* was more likely to have been due to:

(a) A sighting report from another submarine (presumably one lurking nearer the South African coastline).
(b) The submarine having followed the ship on the surface, and working ahead in the prevailing low visibility.
(c) The submarines, having failed to find traffic lanes, were spread on a line of bearing to intercept, and *Orcades'* tormentor was the one furthest to the southwest.

That disposed only of the specific allegations in respect to the sinking of the *Orcades*. There was still the more general question of security in South Africa to consider. The Director of Trade Division (DTD), B.M. Schofield, believed that a full enquiry into shipping security generally in the Union should be held. Reports had been received from time to time concerning leaks of information and the DTD had never been able to get to the bottom of it, and wanted an end to an unsatisfactory state of affairs. The DNI, however, recognised that such an enquiry would be "an extremely wide and vexed question, confused by considerable political difficulties". For the Union authorities resented any interference from the Imperial government and would be unlikely to accept the setting-up of an Admiralty committee under the DTD's nominee, Admiral Tottenham, who would have to be sent out from the UK. Early in 1942 the Union Government had accepted Colonel William Webster of the Security Service (and attached to the British Military Mission) as Security Liaison Officer in Pretoria to advise generally on security matters. Although he lacked executive authority, he did persuade the Union government to appoint four South African security officers at their major ports. But such moves had limited effect. The wider issue of the enemy's intelligence system within South Africa was receiving special consideration at this time. Indeed, General Smuts was said to be currently very "shipping security minded", and though this was said to be "largely for political reasons (Portuguese East Africa)", yet

The South African Connection

"at a later date it might be possible to take the question of S. African domestic security on to the highest plane."

While the delicate political situation in South Africa is one to which we shall return, the censoring of the Durban events in the press is the one to which we now turn our attention. The censorship arrangements in South Africa at the time seem to have been based on a voluntary agreement entered into by the British High Commission, the South African Bureau of Information and the newspaper editors. Ship movements naturally featured prominently in such a scheme. Private arrangements between individual editors and specific bodies were also made. Thus Mervyn Ellis, the editor of the *Natal Mercury*, agreed with Brigadier A.G. Salisbury-Jones, head of No. 203 (UK) Military Liaison Mission in South Africa to restrict reporting of the movement of Imperial troops.[8] Normally, however, the British High Commission would request the Bureau of Information to approach newspaper editors to black-out coverage of certain items. A recent example at the time concerned the official evacuation of women and children from Singapore. In a long letter to Salisbury-Jones (which was mostly taken up with the Clairwood courts-martial affair), Ellis pointed out that the Bureau's approach to him arrived too late to prevent the publication of details concerning the evacuation.[9]

Later in November 1942, after the sinking of the *Orcades*, the naval authorities reiterated their demand that silence in respect to sinkings by U-boats should be preserved. This prompted a stinging leader by Ellis in the *Natal Mercury* of November 7, which Harlech's Cape Town representative, Sir E.J. Harding, saw as the culmination of a campaign by newspapers to loosen the restrictions on freedom of the press.[10] The newspapers' representative, Harry Lawrence, had previously spoken to Harding and had apparently intimated that while the newspapers were concerned to observe loyally the understandings on what was permissible to publish, they really wanted to publish statements that the survivors from torpedoed ships who had been landed at Union ports had been well looked after. While Harding felt this would pose no problems for the naval authorities, it seems that Ellis of the *Natal Mercury* wished in general to publish further and better particulars, though not such of course as would endanger shipping security.

Harding later suggested to Rear-Admiral Tait that the latter should write to Ellis, offering to discuss the whole question with him. As Tait was of the opinion that the circulation of the *Natal Mercury* was "only" 10,000, and that it was "read very little in the country districts of Natal", his concern about the activities of Ellis was muted.

The correspondence, referred to previously, between Ellis and Salisbury-Jones concerning the Durban incident, was in fact prompted by a mutual interest in what were considered to be problems of discipline afflicting the British Army in transit in South Africa. The diagnosis and proffered solutions were not, however, shared. Ellis reminded Salisbury-Jones that he was editor of a South African newspaper. His duty was not primarily to protect the British military authorities from possible criticism in the wake of rank-and-file servicemen's protests about transit conditions, but to keep his South African readers informed about relevant events where he judged it politic to do so. Thus local public opinion might force his hand to publish information which the military authorities might prefer not to be disclosed, though he readily recognised that some sensitive military information could not be revealed.

He turned next to the court-martial proceedings which were then taking place, but which of course had not been mentioned in the local newspapers. Ellis reeled off a number of complaints as to why the issue was a matter of local concern (and why, presumably, he was unhappy at suppressing the information; again, presumably, at the instance of the British military authorities). He wrote:

> It is most unfortunate that such a trial should be staged in Durban at this time. The way in which the court has been constituted, turning it into a Field General Court Martial; the rumour that has gone around that the men refused to sail because they were afraid to go to Singapore; allegations about the condition of certain ships, and certain other aspects of the whole affair are creating a bad impression. These things cannot be kept quiet in Durban, which is one of the biggest whispering galleries in the world, and the fact that there has been no newspaper publication of any sort has meant that a whole group of distorted versions of what is happening is going round the town.[11]

Ellis was evidently concerned also about local South African feelings towards the Imperial Forces Transit Camp at Clairwood. South African sensibilities were being tested when the British authorities sought to claim authority over deeds and actions occurring within the confines of a camp which South Africans could not forget was firmly located on South African soil. Ellis insisted that he was enthusiastically in favour of further collaboration with the British military authorities. He understood their problem in conducting a war on so many fronts, and having now to raise a conscript army, as distinct from the volunteer forces which made up the South African Army. A difference in quality of recruits was bound to emerge and the local population could judge this for themselves when Imperial troops arrived in transit:

> The last convoy created a most unfortunate impression. Its bearing and general discipline was bad and I myself can see a marked deterioration in the troops that are now being sent out.

He knew that unflattering confidential reports were being sent to the Union Defence authorities about such matters; more importantly, "There are, at the moment, signs of a criticism of Britain which may develop into something very serious". It was urgent for the British military authorities to avoid creating opportunities for fractious criticism of their deeds among the locals.

Overreaction by the British military authorities to indiscipline was in fact later recognised by some senior officials. Some time after the Clairwood courts-martial, Roger Wilson, an ex-Indian Army officer attached to the Union government, complained to Harding that, "all sorts of trivial cases are in South Africa brought before court martials [sic] which would elsewhere be dealt with by local disciplinary action". Wilson hoped on his tours of the main transit centres to remedy this situation.[12] The Clairwood proceedings and the circumstances giving rise to them were widely known and commented upon, and Ellis remained critical of official attitudes:

> Take, for instance, this Court Martial. After [a] deputation [of the accused] had called on me asking us to report the proceedings, we applied for permission to attend. We were not refused permission to report the proceedings, but we were told that Clairwood Camp was a prohibited area and that our reporters would not be admitted. That raises a very difficult problem with a South African staff, who naturally know what is said and who are in some cases very jealous over what

Durban 1942: A British Troopship Revolt

they may consider to be any attempt by the British authorities to assume in South Africa a control which it is doubtful if they can legally justify.[13]

Salisbury-Jones received Ellis's letter with some puzzlement. On the one hand, Ellis appeared to him to be expressing some criticism of the disciplinary record of British troops in transit. On the other hand, Ellis seemed to think that the courts-martial at Clairwood were somehow inappropriate, in that sympathy for the mutineers' predicament had been widely felt by the civilian population in the district.[14] The probability was that Ellis was primarily concerned to prevent, without resorting to censorship, adverse criticism of British military personnel or military authorities in South Africa which might intensify racial discord between Afrikaaner elements and Imperial troops.

In his letter to Salisbury-Jones, Ellis referred to incidents which had taken place at Pietermaritzburg, the capital of Natal, shortly after the *City of Canterbury* protest had occurred at Durban. As Lord Harlech had earlier described those incidents:

> one of the results of stories about this whole [*City of Canterbury*] affair is the intensification of racial feeling by the alleged aggressiveness of Afrikaner [sic] military police in Pietermaritzburg against Imperial troops stationed at Oribi Camp: in fact, that the whole business, doubtless exaggerated by rumour and ex parte statements, is having a bad effect on relations between Imperial and South African authorities in and around Durban.[15]

It appears that Salisbury-Jones had pressed Ellis to prevent information on this matter appearing in his newspaper. Ellis's response was to cut down his coverage of the incident "to the barest possible limits in view of the public agitation which was growing up. We were being inundated with letters on the matter, which I did not use, and I held my hand as long as I could".[16] His judgment was that to suppress the item would do more harm than good to the Allied cause, the kind of judgment on balance which broadcasters and newspaper editors often reach today in the face of government condemnation, distortion and manipulation.[17]

Thus while racial discord would hardly be welcome to those supporting a united South African front against the Nazis, the

The South African Connection

censoring of information about such discord might likewise be dangerous. It might also play straight into the hands of the Nationalist elements in South African politics who were agitating for South Africa's withdrawal from the struggle against Nazi Germany and in favour of a policy of neutrality towards the war. The spectacle of British military sovereignty being exercised within South African territory might further encourage acts of sabotage by members of the Ossewa Brandweg (OB), the militant wing of the Afrikaaner Nationalist movement which sympathised with the Nazi cause. Ellis did not *explicitly* refer to this connection in his long correspondence with Salisbury-Jones. It was, however, surely what he had in mind when citing the "signs of criticism of Britain which may develop into something very serious", to which we referred earlier. The courts-martial were taking place when the Prime Minister, Field Marshal Smuts, who was committed to the Allied cause, was struggling to maintain his authority against the challenge of those Nationalists, Hertzog and Malan, who wished to declare South African neutrality in the war. Any bad publicity for the British military presence in South Africa would be a bonus to the Nationalist cause. That was why Ellis could express regret at both the perceived display of indiscipline among British troops in transit and at what he considered the insensitive prosecutions of the *City of Canterbury* protesters. In respect of the latter, the gossip among the good citizens of Durban was not unsympathetic to their plight.

Ellis's influence within Durban and among South African members of Parliament, plus his importance as a conduit for informed opinion on matters of significance to the British interest were not underestimated by Lord Harlech, the UK High Commissioner. The latter wrote to Air Commodore Frew at the beginning of February, pointing out that Ellis was due to have lunch with Prime Minister Smuts that day, and that the court-martial business was generating much questioning about the constitutionality of the British military authorities' legal proceedings. Though we have already examined some of the thorny jurisdictional questions arising out of the *City of Canterbury* incident, it was the local population's *perception* of the legality of the proceedings which Ellis evidently found worrying and which prompted Harlech to share his concerns with Frew. Outlining to Frew what he understood to be the essential details as they occurred, he continued:

> So much for the facts that led up to the trouble. Now for the serious side of it. It is being said in Durban that while no doubt the British military authorities can convene a General Court Martial in South Africa, it is illegal for them to convene a "Field" General Court Martial on South African soil and in an area not under a proclamation of martial law without the express approval of the Union legal authorities. It is alleged that the officer convening the court martial had no legal power to do so, or to confirm the findings and that only you or Salisbury-Jones has that power under conditions now obtaining in the Union. It is alleged that Clairwood Camp was declared a prohibited area not by Brigadier Daniel, the Officer Commanding Natal Command, but by a non-South African officer, and that this is irregular.[18]

As Harlech reminded Frew, "South Africa is, of course, very touchy – especially the lawyers – on constitutional questions". He wanted reassurance that the Union authorities had indeed been consulted to ensure that the "procedure for dealing with the unfortunate incidents at Durban are fully legal". What alarmed Harlech was the prospect that convictions, if obtained, might be quashed on review on a jurisdictional technicality. The consequences of this happening were "often most unfortunate", meaning presumably that the illegitimate encroachment on South African legal sovereignty by the British military authorities would be plain for all to see, and could add further fuel to anti-British feeling.

Frew's response to these expressions of concern was to point out that Ellis, "has always caused trouble over military matters", and to indicate that Wing Commander Shurlock, the senior RAF legal officer in Rhodesia, "would not do anything that was not covered by law".[19] Harlech appeared satisfied and observed in reply that the day after Ellis had had a long chat with Smuts, he met Harlech:

> and by that time was much more amenable and calmed down not merely about the court martial but about many other things!
> He is a Welshman born in Llandaff, and being cleverer than most of his fellows in the Durban Club, he picks up all sorts of tales and then works himself up into passions against Governments in general and local "authorities" in particular.[20]

The South African Connection

Anarchistic traits Ellis was unlikely to possess. But there was no mistaking the sensitivity of the situation in South African politics to which Ellis's antennae were more attuned that were Salisbury-Jones's. The latter acknowledged in his autobiography that he had arrived on the South African scene in late 1941 with a simplistic notion of popular feelings:

> Until my arrival in South Africa and my early talks with Smuts I had not a clear insight into the true situation in South Africa nor realised the difficulties which beset Smuts when he became Prime Minister. Hitherto, I had assumed that the whole of South Africa was united in support of the war. Now I realized how wrong I had been and that my own task would not always be easy.[21]

It was apparent that in early 1942 he was still at the learning stage. Leaving aside the "native" (i.e. Bantu), Indian and Cape Coloured populations of South Africa, who respectively totalled about 6.6 million, 220,000 and 770,000 in 1940, Afrikaaners constituted nearly 60 per cent of the two million European population of the country, and the British about 35 per cent.[22] On the other hand, as Ellis's correspondence implies, there was a separate South African identity which had grown among those of British origin. That did not prevent their commitment, as members of the British Empire, to supporting Britain militarily in her struggle against the Axis powers. Nor, of course, were Afrikaaners deterred from pursuing the same aim: after all, the Prime Minister, Smuts, was himself an Afrikaaner who had fought the British during the Boer War.

The problem for Britain was that Smuts' commitment was not shared by all Afrikaaners. Not only the followers of the extreme Nationalist, D.F. Malan (who later became Prime Minister in 1948 and institutionalised the odious system of *apartheid*), but also many of the supporters of the more moderate Nationalist, J.B.M. Hertzog, Prime Minister till supplanted by Smuts in September 1939 when the South African parliament refused to back his call for neutrality, expressed open opposition to South African participation in the war. With Hertzog allied with Malan's Nationalists to form the Herenigde (People's) Party, a policy of republicanism was now pursued, entailing withdrawal from the war and withdrawal from the Empire. More seriously, sympathy with Nazi aims was widely expressed among supporters. When politicians such as Oswald Pirow, who had been Minister of Defence between 1933 and 1939, left the extreme Herenidge Party with the aim of forming a "New Order" Party which advocated a Nazi-style constitution, and when the OB's bomb-planting activities were considered by some as patriotic (but as treasonable by those supporting the war effort against the Axis powers),[23] the delicate political situation in South Africa was underlined.

Among Smuts' party members, both Afrikaaner and British in origin, there were those who lent him their support for his domestic policies of modest social reform only because they were frightened of the efforts of the radical wing of the New Orderers in the Opposition to exploit the economic discontents of the enfranchised poor whites for republican or Nazi purposes.[24] Such backing for Smuts' line could not afford to be alienated. Given the fragility of support for Smuts' pro-war stance, it is clear that provocation and encouragement of anti-British sentiment could come from any quarter. If British troops in transit were seen as over-boisterous, arrogant and undisciplined, then public opinion among South Africans might shift. By the same token, if the British military authorities, in an endeavour to stamp hard on what they took to be insubordination, were thought by the local population both to have over-reacted and to have displayed insensitivity to questions of South African sovereignty and to feelings of South African identity, by conducting trials on South African soil based on *British* law, then popular alienation from the Allied cause might likewise be provoked. Ellis, with his hand firmly on the local pulse, and with an appreciation of the brittle nature of South African politics in respect to the war, recognised this.

The organisation of the South African Defence Forces (SADF) reflected the delicate political balance existing among the white population of the country.[25] When South Africa entered the war, Smuts decided to raise a Mobile Defence Force in which volunteers offered to serve "anywhere in Africa", as Pirow and his followers had threatened opposition if existing regiments were sent beyond the borders of the Union.[26] A new oath was later administered to enable South African soldiers to serve in *any* theatre of war, and not just in Africa. Yet by March 1943, it was reported by Lord Harlech that only 30–40 per cent of the rank-and-file of the 1st S.A. Division, back home on leave from Egypt, had agreed to this wider commitment. Harlech saw this as part of a larger development in South Africa at this time. There was, he reported, "a general lowering of tempo of the Union's war consciousness and war effort", which he attributed to a number of causes, but which was also reflected in a lowering of morale in the SADF and in an "impression of muddle, indecision and incompetence at Defence Headquarters in Pretoria".[27]

Perhaps Ellis's earlier strictures about British military personnel when contrasted with their South African counterparts were precipitate. Yet the dilemma for those agitating for the Allied cause in the war was that "war-mindedness" among South Africans had to be continuously cultivated: in order to aid military recruitment; to use South African ports militarily; to promote war production; to encourage charitable donations and fund-raising for the war effort; and to discourage conspicuous consumption. On the other hand, war "action" could pose the threat of stimulating a political *reaction* by the disaffected elements favouring neutrality or even the Nazi cause *tout court*. In early 1942, Ellis believed that the balance was dangerously poised and saw the courts-martial as provocative. A year later the Malan and Pirow factions still posed a threat to South African war participation, and the general election due in 1943 would be a key battle, especially since:

> To pretend that the Smuts Government is popular would be idle. Smuts has "prestige" and admiration rather than popularity or affection in South Africa. His colleagues – collectively – are now definitely unpopular and most have outstayed their welcome in the public mind.[28]

Yet Harlech was confident that Malan and Pirow would fail to remove Smuts from office. That may have been because the ardour of the neutrality campaign had cooled as the direct military threat to South Africa receded. For once North Africa had been rendered safe, Madagascar secure, the Japanese tied up in the Solomons, convoys less frequent, air raids a remote possibility, and the 1st S.A. Division back on leave from Egypt, Imperial war consciousness (and its antithesis, sympathy for the Nazi cause) became less pervasive in the public mind. In early 1942, at the time of the *City of Canterbury* troubles, the picture had been very different.

Chapter 7

Like Other Mutinies?

In a recent book, Lawrence James has sought to identify the characteristics of different types of mutiny.[1] His general approach is to classify them according to the *forms* of mutiny, the *methods* of the mutineers and *reactions of officialdom*. With particular reference to mutinies among British and Commonwealth forces between 1797 and 1956, he notes that their frequency increased during periods of wartime conscription, as civilians strove with difficulty to adjust to "compliance and quietism". Yet while mutiny activism was observed between 1797 and 1801 during the Revolutionary Wars and between 1917 and 1920 during the First World War, it was not so marked (though it did occur) during the Second World War. By then the service chiefs had become more aware of the importance of good conditions and of maintaining morale. Those servicemen whom psychiatrists found wanting for service duties would simply be returned to civilian life.

James's conclusion was that mutinies were *not* typified by a *Bounty*-like uprising, which he accurately analysed as mass desertion from an oppressive regime. Nor, with the odd exception, were they inspired by political motives, though some mutinies during the Second World War involved Empire troops who "defected" to the Japanese. Rather, most mutinies were "humdrum affairs", in which servicemen lodged collective protests against unbearable conditions and sought redress for their grievances:

> Complaints were invariably confined to injuries which had their causes in the everyday routines of service life. Overwork, unpalatable or inadequate rations, the removal of privileges, the imposition of new burdens, uncomfortable accommodation, heartless officers and NCOs, vindictive and excessive punishments, low wages and, in earlier periods, slowness in their payment, were the commonest sources of discontent and mutiny.[2]

Durban 1942: A British Troopship Revolt

The methods of mutineers, he found, frequently reflected the methods of protest in civilian life. Servicemen who collectively disobeyed orders were "going on strike". Thus in the case of the *City of Canterbury*, we can perceive that the walk-off was equivalent to a walk-out from the factory. Where officers offered crude and uncompromising responses to servicemen's truculence, they often succeeded only in transforming sullenness into mutiny.

It will be recalled that the definition of "mutiny" in force during the Second World War was taken to mean collective insubordination or a combination by two or more persons to resist (or induce others to resist) lawful service authority. In fact the Army Act 1881 and the annual Air Force Act then in force did not in terms define "mutiny" statutorily. The then current *Manual of Military Law* and *Manual of Air Force Law* both *suggested* the above definition in their notes to the relevant Section 7. So long as that definition was endorsed by the Judge Advocate General, it was effectively binding on courts-martial;[3] it was approved specifically by Lord Goddard in *R. v. Grant* (1957), heard in the Courts-Martial Appeal Court which was set up in 1951.

Ironically, by the time of the judgment in *Grant*, the relevant Army and Air Force Acts had been repealed by the Army Act 1955 and the Air Force Act 1955, following the report of a House of Commons select committee into service law. The new acts both offer a common statutory definition of mutiny in Section 31(3) of each act. Mutiny now meant:

> a combination between two or more persons subject to service law, or between persons two at least of whom are subject to service law:
>
> (a) To overthrow or resist lawful authority in Her Majesty's forces . . .
> (b) To disobey such authority in such circumstances as to make the disobedience subversive of discipline, or with the object of avoiding any duty or service against, or in connection with operations against, the enemy, or
> (c) to impede the performance of any duty or service in Her Majesty's forces. . . .

In one respect, this definition appears to equivocate over the meaning of "mutiny" by referring to the "overthrow" of, as an alternative to resistance to, lawful authority. For whereas "overthrow" suggests the

Like Other Mutinies?

finality of casting off the service shackles, "resistance" could well be a mere temporary device. The other provisions, in particular, subsection (c), appear to envisage even a minor collective disruption of service routine as constituting a mutiny. This is an expansive definition.

Whether before or after 1955, the service authorities were required only to demonstrate, on the part of alleged mutineers, a collective resistance to lawful service authority. It was (and remains) unnecessary to go further and to establish a permanent repudiation of such authority, either *in toto* or in respect to particular orders. As to total repudiation, the "Mutiny on the *Bounty*" is, of course, the classic instance. On two occasions during the Napoleonic Wars, British ships were forcibly taken over by their crews and were sailed into French ports. One ship was the frigate HMS *Danae*, whose cruiser namesake was involved in escort duties with the *City of Canterbury* during her Far East exploits in 1942.[4]

In the Second World War collective insubordination, leading to "defections" to the enemy, occurred on very few occasions and involved Commonwealth troops. The most serious case (in view of the punishments carried out) concerned 15 mobilised soldiers of the Ceylon Defence Force who were tried by FGCM in the Cocos-Keeling Islands in May 12–16 1942. A few days earlier they had attempted to seize the battery by force, prompted by pro-Japanese and anti-European sentiments. The attempt failed, but one British officer was wounded and one loyal Sinhalese killed. At the court-martial four men were acquitted of all the charges, but the others were found guilty of one or other of the mutiny charges put. Seven men were sentenced to death (four later commuted) and three were hanged in Colombo in July 1942.[5]

A comparable incident occurred on Christmas Island in March 1942, when a number of Indians of the 7th Gold Coast Regt., the Hong Kong and Singapore Royal Artillery, attacked their CO, Captain Williams, and the British NCOs of their unit. On March 4, after a bombardment of the island by the Japanese, a white flag was hoisted. But on March 11, before the Japanese had actually landed, Captain Williams and the NCOs were attacked and killed by the Indians, apparently with a view to the latter ingratiating themselves with the Japanese. After the war these men were tracked down and court-martialled in Singapore for having joined in a mutiny. Of the seven prosecuted in 1947, five were sentenced to hang, one was acquitted and the sentence not confirmed in the case of the seventh. While the findings and sentences of death were confirmed by the King, representations were made by the governments of India and Pakistan and the sentences were subsequently commuted to penal servitude for life.[6]

While collective "defections" to the enemy during the Second World War were extremely rare (omitting the cases of the Indian National Army, recruited, initially, from prisoners captured by the Japanese, and the Indian Liberation Army, recruited to fight for Germany from POWs captured in North Africa),[7] instances of resistance to the undertaking of military duties against targets or enemies with whom servicemen sympathised are best illustrated by the case of the British soldiers refusing to fight against the Bolsheviks in North Russia in 1919. The more prosaic demand for early demobilisation did, however, sharpen the opposition of the soldiers to the orders issued to them.[8] Another ostensibly political mutiny was that of the Connaught Rangers in the Punjab in 1920, in protest at British policy in Ireland. The apparently mirror-image Curragh Incident in 1914 was, of course, far short of being a mutiny. No officer who threatened to resign his commission if ordered to enforce Home Rule was, in the event, faced with such a choice.[9]

As previously indicated, the typical mutiny was a modest, undramatic affair, revolving around grievances about service conditions. Even the notable Salerno mutiny in September 1943, when 300 men from the 50th Division and the 51st Highland Division refused to join the divisions to which they had been posted as part of reinforcements to the Salerno beachhead, was linked to organisational failings at HQ. The men had been convalescing in Tripoli after the Sicily campaign in July and August 1943, and had been expecting to be repatriated to the UK in order to train for the D-Day landings. Instead they were, apparently erroneously, boarded on ships bound for Salerno, where they disembarked. Ordered to join the 46th Division, 300 out of the detachment of 1,500 refused, insisting on returning to their own divisions, the 50th and 51st. That was no longer possible and those holding out, now down to 191, were court-martialled. Three sergeants were sentenced to death, five corporals were sentenced to be reduced

Like Other Mutinies?

to the ranks and ten years' penal servitude, and the privates received seven years' penal servitude. The death sentences were commuted on confirmation to twelve years' penal servitude and reduction to the ranks, and all sentences were suspended[10].

The following cases of mutiny between 1939 and 1949, in which sentences of death (later commuted) were passed, emphasise just how seriously the service authorities were prepared to treat incidents which, to the layman's eyes, might appear trivial.[11] In all these cases, as indicated previously, the mutinies can without understatement be attributed to such prosaic causes as boredom, unimaginative military routine, general lack of basic comforts or even facilities, poor interpersonal relations and the effects of drink. Thus, in June 1940, four men forming a post in the forward area at Mersa Matruh in the Middle East had consumed too much alcohol. They shut up the NCO in charge in a pill box and assaulted their CO on his rounds. Charged with joining in a mutiny, they were all convicted. One was sentenced to death by firing squad, two to ten years' penal servitude and the fourth to seven years. The court made a recommendation to mercy in the case of the first man:

> on the grounds that, with seven years of Army service, his character before this offence was very good, and that the evidence shows that a certain amount of intoxicating liquor had been consumed just prior to the offence being committed.

As a consequence, his death sentence was commuted to fourteen years' penal servitude.

In December 1942, in North Africa, a soldier became violent and abusive during a rail journey. The RSM ordered three men to tie him up, but they refused. He then ordered four others to do so. The accused said, "Refuse to do it; the others have". As a result, they also refused. The outcome was that he was court-martialled on December 31, charged *inter alia*, with causing a mutiny:

> in that he, in the Field, on 8th December 1942, addressed soldiers of the mortar platoon of his battalion in mutinous language, advising them to refuse an order given to them to tie him up.

He was sentenced to death but the sentence was commuted on confirmation to twenty months imprisonment, to be served in the Command. In the event the finding on the mutiny charge was quashed by the Secretary of State, on the ground that the particulars of the charge did not allege that a mutiny was actually caused. Convictions under the Army Act, Sections 8 and 9, were, however, confirmed.[12]

In Italy, in late January 1944, five men had been held in close arrest in the guard room when they were ordered to parade for porterage duties up the line. They all refused. Tried for mutiny, they were all found guilty and sentenced to death, though the sentences, on confirmation, were commuted to seven years' penal servitude.

Finally, four soldiers of the 1st Battalion, the Mauritius Regiment, were charged with mutiny in Madagascar in December 1943. The Battalion had arrived from Mauritius on December 20 and had displayed symptoms of being "browned off" at having to be sent out of Mauritius. The company commanders ordered P.T. parades at 0630 hours on December 22 and a large number of the men refused to turn out. After a court-martial, one man was sentenced to death by being shot, a second was sentenced to fourteen years' penal servitude, a third received 12 years' penal servitude and a fourth seven years. The death sentence was commuted on confirmation to fifteen years' penal servitude, and the other sentences were also commuted on confirmation.

In all these examples, the original imposition of the death sentence attests to an official attitude, within the Army during the war, of maximum severity in sentencing, moderated eventually by a considered, perhaps systematic, application of discretion in reducing punishments; parallel, it might be thought, to the enforcement of the Bloody Code of eighteenth-century criminal law. Measured against the sentences originally meted out in the above cases, the punishments imposed on the Durban offenders were modest.

The circumstances, of course, also differed in their particulars. For none of the above examples arose from conditions aboard ship. Yet recently Bill Glenton has provided a vivid, sardonic account of how he and his fellow lower deckers, both regulars and "Hostilities Only", in one wartime naval vessel, went (or were driven) over the edge and staged an inevitably short-lived shipboard mutiny in 1944.[13] The landing ship, HMS *Lothian*, contemptuously nicknamed by the crew *Loathsome*, made up one unit of Force X, planned as a US Navy-led task force to invade the Philippines. The senior British commander, Admiral A.G. Talbot, insisted during the long

Like Other Mutinies?

voyage to the rendezvous point in the most searing tropical heat, on observing:

> ... the kind of "bullshit" routine found in battleships or training establishments. Morning "Divisions" and "Evening Quarters" were introduced – formalities that took no account of our physical problems and proved just an extra irritation. But what annoyed us more was that only the seamen and not the other ratings had to endure them.

Thus they were forced to struggle into their stifling working uniforms for inspection and then change back immediately into their more comfortable overalls. Having crossed the Tropic of Cancer, they were dismayed that the tropical routine of stand-easy during the energy-sapping heat of the afternoons was not to be implemented. No tropical clothing was aboard ship, apart of course from that worn by the officers. *Lothian's* own CO, Captain Petrie was, the men felt, overawed by Admiral Talbot's presence, though the captain was, technically, in command of his own vessel.

While the ventilation system was on its last legs, "our purgatory was an aphrodisiac for the ship's wildlife". For troops in transit to complain of cockroaches and rats in abundance was one thing. For seasoned sailors to do likewise indicated the magnitude of the crawling invasion, as the insects and vermin penetrated every crevice and food receptacle. The fresh vegetables and tinned fruit that the crew had hauled aboard the ship while in dock in New York were nowhere to be seen in the mess. There was no doubting, however, which members of the ship's complement were tucking into luscious meals. When the limited supply of drinking water, foul though it was, also dried up due to a major fault with the evaporators (which removed the salt), there was consternation. When they discovered that, notwithstanding, Admiral Talbot had been taking daily baths in fresh water, their anger increased.

On September 1 1944 the ship was about to leave Balboa in Panama to continue her voyage to the South-West Pacific. At that point talk of action began to circulate surreptitiously in the messes. At stand-easy the tension rose, as the ODs looked to the ABs and killicks to start something. Yet "No one appeared over-concerned about whether it would succeed – an unlikely prospect – let alone the certain severe punishment that would follow". Then, after work resumed, the three principal agitators, as Glenton himself described them, triggered the protest by walking boldly down the gangway, straight into the US canteen. Soon a:

> deafening crescendo of noise arose as men bellowed out their support and began hammering mess tables as though they were a form of tribal drum.

Various attempts by petty officers and officers, using both persuasion, threats of mutiny charges and the bringing up of the Marines, failed to get the ratings out of their mess deck and back to their duties. Instead of instant compliance with Admiral Talbot's instruction to the First Lieutenant to order the Marines to fire into the open hatches, the hatches were shut tight over the men's heads. The ratings were now deprived of food, light and adequate drinking water or ventilation in an unbearably cramped and stuffy messdeck. The inevitable questioning and bickering began among themselves, with fears even expressed about their survival, given the ever-diminishing supply of oxygen. Capitulation soon followed, in order to end their misery below decks. Seventeen of the more senior crew were court-martialled and reduced in rank, the three ringleaders naturally being the most severely punished. The remainder, mainly young and inexperienced, were dealt with summarily. Bill Glenton was one of these. All received six months punishment drill and six months extra duties. In the suffocating conditions of New Guinea, which they had now reached, it was no light punishment to labour while the rest of the crew relaxed during the afternoon stand-easy.

The causes of the mutiny can plainly be located in the oppressive conditions, both physical and psychological, in which the men were expected to undertake their duties. Tropical conditions did not result in tropical routines, while other indicators of discomfort, such as the unpalatable food and the want of drinking water, might not by themselves have provoked a mutiny. What perhaps pushed the men over the edge was the feeling of relative deprivation. They knew that adequate quantities of wholesome food were on board. Had they not sweated to load it aboard at New York? They knew that the trickle of foul drinking water was not the sole supply aboard the vessel. Had they not been told of Admiral Talbot's bath arrangements? No doubt they recognised differential standards of facilities within the Navy

Like Other Mutinies?

according to rank. But surely, they must have thought, the gap should not have been *that* wide? The *Lothian* affair has been discussed at some length, partly because it typifies the mutiny which is a plea for better treatment, precisely the claim advanced by those who left the *City of Canterbury*. A further, coincidental, observation can be made. HMS *Lothian* was commissioned into the Royal Navy in 1944, leaving the Senior Service in 1946. Her original identity was the *City of Edinburgh*, a sister ship of the *City of Canterbury*.[14]

The connection between the mutiny on the *Lothian* and the *City of Canterbury* may indeed have been purely coincidental, but we can explore in more detail the extent to which the Durban affair may have been similar to, or even connected with, other instances of servicemen's unrest within the same environment, incidents which might have been precipitated, broadly speaking, by the same factors underlying the *City of Canterbury* protest on January 12–13 1942. By "environment", we mean problems connected, first, with conditions aboard the *City of Canterbury* and similar troopers operating from Durban; and secondly, the general disposition and attitude of servicemen, especially RAF personnel, based or in transit in South Africa.

During the disturbance on the quayside at Point Docks in the early morning of January 13 servicemen from other troopships, which were in port at the time, joined in the *City of Canterbury* protest. W/Cdr. Shurlock indeed stated that there were four troopers regularly docking at Durban which were reputed to be sub-standard in terms of facilities for the servicemen travelling on them. A driver in the Royal Army Service Corps, T.E. Gower, recalls that after arriving at Durban off the *Andes* in convoy WS 14, he spent four days at Clairwood Camp while awaiting transport to the Middle East. When these particular ships arrived and his draft were returned to the docks for embarkation, a repeat of the events involving the *City of Canterbury* occurred, that is a general walk-off from the ships, only this time accompanied by some officers. On this occasion senior officers asked the protesters to nominate spokesmen to present their grievances, while insisting that meanwhile everyone else should board the vessels. A return aboard ship then took place, but instead of discussions with the men's spokesmen commencing, the ships were moved away from the quayside. Nothing more was heard of the "spokesmen", and the ships eventually made for the Persian Gulf and Iraq, via Trincomalee and

Durban 1942: A British Troopship Revolt

Bombay. Mr. Gower, who himself now lives in Natal, South Africa is insistent that the *City of Canterbury* was not one of the ships involved. Yet the incident certainly must have occurred within days of that confrontation.

The most uncanny parallel, however, was when 1,000 RAF men walked off the *Empire Woodlark* at Durban on August 15 1942.[15] Again the ship's condition was condemned and a rumour even circulated that, due to its unseaworthiness, many of the crew had signed off. Nonetheless, officers managed to coax the servicemen back on board after many hours. The next morning, as the ship was thought to be about to move to anchorage to await replacement crew, thus apparently confirming the rumour, around 50 servicemen scrambled down to the quayside. After more negotiations, 30 returned, while the remainder were lined up before senior officers. Name, rank and number, together with paybook, were taken, and they were informed of the dire consequences of disobeying the order to board ship for India. They were then left in the charge of one sergeant who chatted with them for some time before he was summoned to the ship's gangway. He returned, smiling, to announce that *everyone* was being taken off the ship and returned to Clairwood. The camp C.O. called them a "disgrace", and five weeks later, they went to India on board other vessels. Lord Haw Haw referred to the *Empire Woodlark* mutiny in a broadcast, which perhaps underlined Durban's "whispering gallery" reputation.

Another instance concerns the New Zealand troopship, the *Oorangi* which had sailed in an earlier WS convoy to Durban from Glasgow in early November 1941. James Merrett of Lochgelly remembers the uncomfortable conditions aboard her which he and his fellow-RAF personnel endured. On trans-shipment at Durban, they were to board the *Nieuw Amsterdam* where they had been promised cabins and good conditions for the onward journey to the Middle East. Once again they were put down in the bottom of the ship, where Italian POWs had been kept, and, as in the later incidents, they all landed again off the troopship. Their revolt lasted only about two hours. After being lectured to by their officers and being threatened by a South African Army unit whose weaponry was evidently taken quite seriously, they soon marched backed on board.

The *City of Canterbury* herself experienced another disturbance in

Like Other Mutinies?

April 1942 prior to a trip from Bombay to Colombo. She was carrying the ground staff of No. 413 Squadron, Royal Canadian Air Force (which flew Catalinas) and of No. 22 Squadron, RAF (Beauforts). The Canadians took great exception to the quality of the food prepared for them by Lascar cooks aboard the ship, and led apparently by a pilot officer, flying officer and senior NCOs, walked off the ship. They were soon joined by RAF and naval personnel who were also aboard her. Eventually a Canadian officer came ashore to negotiate with his men, and though the dialogue was seemingly quite threatening an agreement was hammered out. A complete reissue of rations would be brought on board and the Canadians would do the cooking! No disciplinary action was apparently taken against the airmen, though a minor squabble occurred between a chief petty officer and one of the seamen coming back aboard.[16]

India was also the venue of a walk-off by airmen from another troopship. On January 17 1942, a few days after the *City of Canterbury* mutiny, an RAF draft, which included Cpl. L.E. Ransom, an MT driver, landed at Karachi from Bombay, but stayed at Drigh Road for only a week before being taken back to the docks. There they boarded the *Varela*, and three days later were back in Bombay, glad that the short journey was over.

> We were crowded into a small space below decks. The small bread ration we were issued with each morning, was the last resting place of countless oven-baked weevils and as soon as you put it on the shelf above you, dozens of tiny ants took possession of it. As for cockroaches, there were so many that I was convinced they must be part owners of this flea bitten tub.[17]

There is a depressing familiarity in this account which matches closely the descriptions of life aboard other troopships in the Indian Ocean and South Atlantic Stations. But for Cpl. Ransom worse was to come. After journeying to Madras, the draft were taken to the docks and boarded the *Ellenga*. This "rusting hulk" was even worse than the *Varela*, and immediately provoked a walk-off. The Riot Act was read to them but had little effect, especially as they had the backing of senior NCOs, both Army and RAF. The old hand-pumps were broken and the conditions below decks were unfavourably compared to those aboard prison ships. There was a certain elation among the protesters.

Durban 1942: A British Troopship Revolt

"We all thoroughly enjoyed this illegitimate tilt at authority . . . We knew they couldn't bung us all in gaol." The NCOs managed to extract a commitment that the pumps would be repaired and that the draft could sleep on the officers' deck. The business concluded, the men trooped back on board. Cpl. Ransom had no illusions about the limited aims of their action but acknowledged that others might see it differently:

> Our "mutiny", which one dock side "Poonah wallah" insisted on calling it, was a good humoured and not unreasonable protest and nothing more. We were on active service and quite prepared to "rough it", but we had already discovered during our short time in India, that there were still a few "Colonel Blimps" about, who still treated lower ranks as if they belonged to Kipling's Army, deserving no better treatment than the poorest Indian peasant.

This was the crux of the differences in perspective. It was inconceivable to officers, and no doubt to most servicemen, that the latter should "bargain" over their physical conditions. On the other hand it was surely inconceivable to servicemen, and no doubt to most officers, that the latter should abdicate their responsibility for ensuring the maximum level of comfort in passage that it was possible to attain. It is plainly trite to observe that on many occasions expectations were not met, leading to the kinds of outcome which we have been analysing.

A couple of final observations may be made. First, irrespective of conditions aboard troopships docking in South Africa (or even India), were servicemen in this theatre, and RAF personnel in particular, unusually disposed towards indiscipline? The stories of drunkenness among Australian troops are of course legion; which tells us nothing about the accuracy of the claims. Allegations of indiscipline, even if substantiated, may relate to individual "misbehaviour", rather than to "collective insubordination", the essence of mutiny during the war. Any perusal of statistics of offences under military law will reveal that many servicemen are court-martialled or are dealt with summarily every year. During the last war, in view of the vastly increased size of the Armed Forces, statistics were correspondingly high, reflecting also the high intake of conscripts from civilian life to fight alongside regular servicemen (see Tables, 1–3). Officers as well as men were liable to commit offences against military law. R.S. Gordon-Brown, the RAF administrative officer at Clairwood Camp, recalls that a senior officer on the camp staff was tried for drinking too much at a party in the Sergeant's Mess. So, too, was a squadron leader who struck the OC Troops aboard a troopship, and also an officer who did not properly account for an imprest cash account on his arrival in Australia after retreating from the Far East.

Was there a broader climate of indiscipline among RAF personnel in transit? This was the question put by Lord Harlech, the British High Commissioner to South Africa, to his Cape Town representative, Sir E.J. Harding, in July 1942.[18] The latter's own knowledge extended only to instances of drunkenness and petty theft among a few servicemen in Cape Town. But he reported the view of an official at Pollsmoor Barracks that RAF discipline there was unsatisfactory. This was,

> chiefly because practically all the officers were interested in flying and in aeroplanes and in those only. Consequently, they took no interest in keeping the "other ranks" disciplined and happy. An Army captain serving at Pollsmoor, with whom I also talked, confirmed that the discipline among the NCOs and others who stayed at the camp, when on their way back to England to get commissions or because they had finished their training, was far from what it should be.

These are all very vague accusations whose probative value is not high and which do not distinguish between different forms of misconduct, ranging from innocent pranks to the overthrow of lawful authority. In other words, the argument that RAF servicemen in, or passing through, South Africa were predisposed to indiscipline, let alone to rebelliousness, seems wholly untenable. The Durban mutineers, in short, were not looking for trouble, although it will remain a matter of controversy whether their walk-off from the *City of Canterbury*, let alone their failure to reboard her, can be defended or excused.

The second concluding observation, which may not be unconnected with the view that the Durban protesters were not looking for an excuse to leave the ship, relates to the question of politics. The Afrikaaner dimension has been discussed and it has also been noted that the treatment of blacks by some whites in South Africa disturbed a number of the RAF men being held at Clairwood. Ken Berrecloth, one of those who continued the voyage to the Far East and thence to captivity, recalled in his war memoirs that all troops were advised to

Durban 1942: A British Troopship Revolt

Table 1
(a) Strength of Royal Air Force

Date	At Home	Abroad	Total
1 Sep. 1938	66,682	12,021	78,703
1 Sep. 1939	103,708	14,182	117,890
1 Sep. 1940	354,966	24,101	379,067
1 Sep. 1941	653,726	92,787	746,513
1 Sep. 1942	644,480	232,837	877,317
1 Sep. 1943	653,733	328,705	982,438
1 Sep. 1944	701,349	304,536	1,006,080
1 Sep. 1945	633,349	307,518	940,867
1 Sep. 1946	261,069	117,937	379,006

(b) Royal Air Force: Number of Courts-Martial

Period	At Home	Abroad	Total	Average Number per 1,000 personnel
1 Sep. 1938 to 31 Aug. 1939	191	28	219	2.2
1 Sep. 1939 to 31 Aug. 1940	326	74	400	1.6
1 Sep. 1940 to 31 Aug. 1941	1,434	135	1,569	2.8
1 Sep. 1941 to 31 Aug. 1942	2,610	574	3,184	3.9
1 Sep. 1942 to 31 Aug. 1943	2,550	929	3,479	3.7
1 Sep. 1943 to 31 Aug. 1944	2,323	1,329	3,652	3.7
1 Sep. 1944 to 31 Aug. 1945	2,322	1,546	3,868	4.0
1 Sep. 1945 to 31 Aug. 1946	1,749	934	2,683	4.1

These figures relate to Royal Air Force personnel. Women's Services and a few other small categories are excluded.

Source: Report of the Army and Air Force Courts-Martial Committee 1946, Cmd. 7608, 1949, p. 16.

keep away from the black districts of Durban.[19] Presumably this was a safety warning rather than one cautioning against involvement in South African domestic affairs.

A.P. Wheway, the RAF clerical NCO on the staff of the *City of Canterbury*, remembers that during the disturbance, not only was there one serviceman who had been actively agitating to get the men ashore, but there were also several civilians who mixed with the troops on the dock, and who were clearly displaying their sympathies towards them. They may well have been anti-British Afrikaaners. On

Like Other Mutinies?

Table 2

(a) Strength of Army

Date	At Home	Abroad	Total
1 Sep. 1938	102,789	84,978	187,767
1 Sep. 1939	127,917	96,271	224,188
1 Sep. 1940	1,704,045	154,697	1,858,742
1 Sep. 1941	1,913,621	352,995	2,266,616
1 Sep. 1942	1,816,901	660,708	2,477,609
1 Sep. 1943	1,563,068	1,154,977	2,718,045
1 Sep. 1944	984,212	1,782,599	2,766,811
1 Sep. 1945	1,220,489	1,640,134	2,860,623
1 Sep. 1946	390,557	622,124	1,012,681

(b) Army: Number of Courts-Martial

Period	At Home	Abroad	Total	Average number per 1,000 personnel
1 Sep. 1938 to 31 Aug. 1939	1,178	945	2,123	10.3
1 Sep. 1938 to 31 Aug. 1940	3,795	2,945	6,740	6.5
1 Sep. 1940 to 31 Aug. 1941	23,376	2,137	25,513	12.4
1 Sep. 1941 to 31 Aug. 1942	26,866	5,837	32,703	13.3
1 Sep. 1942 to 31 Aug. 1943	23,110	11,829	34,939	13.1
1 Sep. 1943 to 31 Aug. 1944	21,545	15,238	36,783	13.4
1 Sep. 1944 to 31 Aug. 1945	17,843	31,270	49,113	17.5
1 Sep. 1945 to 31 Aug. 1946	10,094	14,176	24,270	16.9

These figures relate only to Army personnel including Royal Marines when subject to the Army Act. Women's Services, Home Guard and a few other small categories are excluded.

Source: Report of the Army and Air Force Courts-Martial Committee 1946, Cmd 7608, 1949, p. 15.

the other hand, they may well have been from the opposite end of the political spectrum (or indeed representative of no political persuasion at all). The role of Communists in the British Armed Forces during the Second World War has recently been explored in Richard Kisch's fascinating study, *The Days of the Good Soldiers*.[20] His emphasis is not on illegal, subversive activities but on the avenues available for the expression of lower ranks' opinions concerning war aims and the postwar world. The vehicles included the establishment and running of "Forces" Parliaments, in particular, the Cairo Parliament in 1943–4.

Table 3
Convictions for Mutiny in the Army since 1939

Year	Home			Abroad				Death Sentences Passed	Death Sentences Carried out	Death Sentences Commuted
	GCM	DCM	FGCM	GCM	DCM	FGCM	Total			
1939/40	–	–	–	–	–	12	12	–	–	–
1940/41	8	–	–	–	–	4	12	1	–	1
1941/42	5	–	–	86	1	79	171	–	–	–
1942/43	6	–	–	–	–	61	67	8	3	5
1943/44	4	–	–	–	–	344	342	5	–	5
1944/45	–	–	–	6	–	240	246	5	–	5
1945/46	6	–	–	100	–	609	715	–	–	–
1946/47	44	–	–	8	–	41	93	–	–	–
1947/48	4	–	–	35	–	–	39	6	–	6
1948/49	–	–	–	29	–	–	29	–	–	–
1949/50	–	–	–	2	–	–	2	–	–	–
1950/51	7	–	–	8	–	–	15	–	–	–
1951/52	–	–	–	–	–	11	11	–	–	–

Source: S.C. on the Army and Air Force Acts, P.P. 1952–53 (289) III, 629, Appendix A.

Like Other Mutinies?

Emerging from the remit given to the Army Bureau of Current Affairs (ABCA), to move beyond the limited educational objectives of the Army Education Corps, and to provide lectures and debates for the troops, the idea of holding a mock parliament took root in Cairo and was later emulated in Deolali, India, and elsewhere.[21] Since Article 541 of King's Regulations forbade servicemen from participating actively in party politics, the Forces Parliament was deemed by a fiction to take place in the future, after the conclusion of the war.[22] Nonetheless, the hypothetical support for the Labour Party in the Cairo Parliament, which sufficiently alarmed the CO, Brigadier Jack Chrystal, that he arrived with military police and ordered the closure of the Parliament (rejected by 600 votes to one!), provided a reliable guide to what eventually resulted at the General Election of 1945.

There is some evidence that educational initiatives during military service enabled servicemen to become better informed, not only about official war aims, but about wider political issues such as post-war reconstruction, colonialism and imperialism.[23] This latter appreciation may have been more pronounced in the case of those serving in the Indian sub-continent and Africa, particularly among those previously politically aware or active.[24] A related question is whether it was *only* service in the Armed Forces which constituted for the majority a politically radicalising experience, given that, according to one estimate, 80 per cent of servicemen voted Labour in the 1945 General Election, and that most of them, it is claimed, did so as a matter of political conviction.[25] In seeking to answer that question, it has recently been argued that war service by itself did not shape political beliefs.[26] The case which argues for a supposed mental separation of soldiers from civilians cannot withstand the contrary evidence from the Second World War to the effect that social interaction between the two categories was more pronounced than hitherto believed. The values and aspirations of the Home Front would be just as keenly felt by servicemen (though divergences over strikes and protected occupations existed). Thus the politics of domestic society would be reflected among the opinions of servicemen. If the politically-motivated strike during the war was rare or non-existent, the same might be said about politically-connected military offences or misconduct. The Mass Observation survey organisation found extensive political apathy in the Army.[27] That is not to deny that *some* servicemen held strong political opinions and sought to debate and discuss them.

In South Africa, Harding reported to Lord Harlech in July 1942:

> Lastly, I might mention that Major Skaife who is in charge of education work for the troops in and round Cape Town volunteered, a few evenings ago, the observation that most of the members of the RAF whom he had seen were, if not "red", at any rate distinctly "pink".[28]

Whether the political persuasions of the Durban mutineers were "red" or "pink", or even "orange" or "blue" (and statistically speaking the majority were at the time, or shortly thereafter, more likely to be "pink" than any other political colour), it should occasion no surprise that political motives played no part in the actions of those protesters whose views have been obtained. Political education within the Armed Forces was developing apace but politically-inspired mutiny was scarcely known during the war. Despite the inconsistent outcomes of the three sets of court-martial proceedings in Durban, that revolt was just like most other mutinies.[29]

Chapter 8

Conclusions

It remains only to note what befell the servicemen who remained on board the *City of Canterbury* as she steamed out of Durban. They were now embarking upon a 5,000 mile voyage to Singapore via Batavia, and were about to endure experiences which were to have devastating effects on them.

The vessel was initially part of convoy DM 2 (i.e. Durban–Malaya), which also included the *Dunera*, famous (or infamous) for her role in transporting internees during the war and for her schools educational cruises after the war. Soon the *City of Canterbury* joined convoy BM12 (Bombay–Malaya), carrying reinforcements for the 18th Division. The vessels accompanying the *City of Canterbury* were the *Empress of Asia*, the Free French vessel, *Felix Roussel*, a distinctive ship with two false square funnels (she was a motor-driven vessel), the *Plancius* and the *Devonshire*.

Aboard the *City of Canterbury* strenuous efforts were made to complete the cleansing of the ship which had been hastily started in Durban. A fire in a coal-bunker, ignited by spontaneous combustion, was tackled, while extensive provision was made for anti-aircraft protection. Training programmes were devised in case of enemy action, while the escort cruiser *Exeter* signalled that the convoy should be prepared for Japanese air attacks as the convoy approached Singapore. By Thursday February 5, Keppel Harbour was in sight. Air attacks on Singapore had become virtually continuous during hours of daylight in the first days of February, and the dock area was a favourite target for Japanese bombers. At about 1030 27 Japanese aircraft comprising Aichi D3A1 (Val) dive-bombers and Mitsubishi G3M (Nell) twin-engined bombers attacked the ships which were still at anchor. The *Empress of Asia* was sunk, while the *City of Canterbury* suffered damage to her steering gear. Three of those aboard the ship were killed and a number injured. *Felix Roussel* also suffered minor damage and few casualties.

Durban 1942: A British Troopship Revolt

A number of awards for bravery were subsequently granted. Captain Snowling of the *Felix Roussel* received a bar to his Distinguished Service Order while the ship herself was awarded the Croix de Guerre by General de Gaulle. Officers on board the Indian Navy vessel *Sutlej* received awards for their part in the rescue of troops from the burning *Empress of Asia*. More pertinent, perhaps, the navigational skills of Captain Percival aboard the *City of Canterbury* enabled the vessel to dodge the worst of the Japanese attacks and were acknowledged with the award of the Order of the British Empire (OBE), Civil Division. Joe Hetherington received the Member of the British Empire (MBE), Civil Division, while others of the crew were commended for their good services during the attack at Keppel Harbour. After the attack, the ship was directed to a dockside mooring point and cargo began to be unloaded.

As to the troops aboard, in a confusing and constantly changing situation, it was decided that only 150 airmen out of the 1,000 aboard should disembark, in order to make space for women and children evacuees. These men stayed on the island about a week, undertaking general duties until they were evacuated to Batavia aboard the *Empire Star*.

The servicemen of No. 4 Ordnance Store Company were also disembarked at Singapore, decamping at Marlborough Barracks. With the British Army in retreat in Malaya, the company could make no real contribution to the maintenance of ordnance supplies. It very shortly ceased to exist as an independent unit and its complement were dispersed to different venues on the island. The surrender of Singapore on February 15 meant that captivity over the next three-and-a-half years become the fate of most of the company. Many did not survive the ordeal, as forced labour on railway construction took its toll. Only a handful managed to effect an escape before the surrender of the island. Sergeant Ron Clayton and a few others took a sampan to reach an island off Sumatra, whence they were evacuated with other escapees under a scheme organised by Colonel Alan Ferguson and operated by the remarkable Ivan Lyon.[1] They eventually reached Colombo and safety.

A number of airmen actually *joined* the *City of Canterbury* at Singapore. They included remnants of No. 151 Maintenance Unit based on the island, who were to be transferred to Batavia; No. 1 Aerodrome

Conclusions

Construction Unit (Unit 24) of the Royal New Zealand Air Force which was to return home; members of No. 453 (Australian) Squadron flying Buffalos; and members of local volunteer units. Supplementing these were an unspecified number of civilian evacuees, some Australian military nurses and even a few deserters.

Batavia was to be the next port of call. The voyage was tense, as the casualty rate for ships making for Java was extremely high.[2] The port area of Tandjong Priok resembled that of Singapore in the sense that disorganised chaos reigned, with goods, equipment and motor vehicles all piled or parked higgeldy-piggeldy. Disembarkation commenced but was interrupted by an air raid which caused little damage. Some of those disembarking were RAF evacuees from Singapore who were to constitute a new Rear Headquarters party to be based in Java. But the numbers of airmen reaching Java now exceeded requirements and many of them in turn were put aboard vessels for Colombo and India. Some members of No. 151 Maintenance Unit, for example, boarded the *Orcades* which took them to Colombo.

The 1,000 or so airmen who had sailed in the *City of Canterbury* from Durban were also disembarked at Batavia. Buitenzorg (now Bogon) was the first location for nearly all of this draft before they were split up into different parties and sent out to various parts of Java. The Japanese were, however, advancing from both east and west of the island and those airmen who did not manage to reach the southern port of Tjilatjap found themselves cut off and captured. Their experiences in captivity were, of course, shocking, whether engaged in airfield repair, railway construction, coal-mining or factory or dock work on behalf of the Japanese.[3]

Very few of this draft of airmen succeeded in evading capture. Of those who did, such as William Batchelor and Bernard Finch, escape was on board the auxiliary destroyer HMS *Kedah*, which sailed from Tjilatjap to Colombo. She had previously evacuated personnel from Singapore on February 10 1942 in the company of HMS *Durban* which was escorting the merchant ship *Empire Star* to Batavia. The latter was carrying among her passengers 135 Australian soldiers who had apparently deserted and who had pushed their way aboard after a confrontation with Captain T.K.W. Atkinson, the captain of Singapore Dockyard. There was a burst of gunfire and Captain Atkinson fell dying. The Australians then boarded the vessel, expecting passage to Australia.[4] In fact, the ship docked at Tandjong Priok after having come under air attack during the voyage and the deserters were soon rounded up by naval personnel from HMS *Durban*.

A handful of ex-*City of Canterbury* airmen, who had originally disembarked at Singapore and had now arrived at Tandjong Priok aboard the *Empire Star*, spent some days on Java before being evacuated to Colombo on February 27. They included John Nevin and W.F. Clark, who subsequently were given further postings to No. 301 Maintenance Unit at Drigh Road in Sind province. Ironically this is where some of the *City of Canterbury* mutineers were sent around this time. Yet for every John Nevin, W.F. Clark, William Batchelor, Bernard Finch or Ron Clayton who sailed on the *City of Canterbury* from Durban to Singapore and who avoided capture by the Japanese, there were hundreds of others who were not so fortunate. The cruel treatment inflicted on Allied POWs and well-documented in numerous publications was shared by those who came off the *City of Canterbury*, either at Singapore or at Batavia. The abominable "medical" experimentation on Allied prisoners by the Japanese, which has only recently come to light, adds a further dimension to the story of ill-treatment in the name of the late Emperor Hirohito. It is also well-known that the survival rate of prisoners of war in Japanese hands was considerably lower than that of prisoners in German camps. A casualty rate of 27 per cent contrasts with a 4 per cent rate among those in German or Italian hands.[5] For approximately every eight survivors from No. 4 OSC mentioned in the narrative, two did not return, such as RSM True, Pte. W.J. Bourne, Pte. L.J. Griffiths or Pte. Leonard Ralph. The last-named died of beri-beri and jungle ulcers on November 22 1943 at Kami-Sonkrai Camp on the Burma–Siam railway. Yet his nephew, Les Paine, of St. Mary's Bay, Kent, who has been trying since the end of the war to piece together the events surrounding his death, is only now, fifty years after the event, getting nearer the truth of the circumstances of his uncle's death.

A parallel story of death and survival can also be told of the RAF units on board the *City of Canterbury*, but it is of importance to observe that release from Japanese captivity at the end of the war frequently did not result in a full recovery of health. When George Paterson, one of the RAF draft disembarking at Batavia in 1942, died in 1982, he was the same weight, a mere six-and-a-half stones, as when he returned from

Conclusions

captivity. Wilfred Parish of Norwich, an aircraftman wireless operator, survived the prison camps on Amboina, but his health was shattered by the ordeal right up to his death in 1988.

The subsequent career of the *City of Canterbury* herself can be briefly recounted. After the dramas of Durban, Singapore and Batavia, she sailed for Colombo on February 12 1942, arriving there with refugees and nearly 500 naval ratings nine days later. Continuing to Bombay, she underwent refitting over a six-week period. Captain Percival handed over command to Joe Hetherington and the *City of Canterbury* was later employed on further duties, including the exchange and repatriation of Allied civilians for Japanese personnel. Extensive trooping duties involving different destinations occupied her time until she was called upon to assist in Operation Husky, the invasion of Sicily in July 1943. In October 1943 she was involved in carrying troops to Naples which had been captured from enemy hands. On May 11 1944 she returned to her home port, Glasgow, in preparation for the Normandy invasion, and on D-Day, June 6, she set off in convoy to the Normandy beaches ("Gold" sector) and disembarked troops off Arromanches. Despite a collision with a landing craft, she returned to Southampton to embark American infantry personnel and sailed in convoy on June 16. Her troops were disembarked and she now made for Glasgow and was released from "Special Operations" on July 11, under the command of Captain Ralph Longstaff.

Returning to the Indian Ocean sector in January 1945, where she spent the remaining months of the war against Japan, she was preparing to join an invasion force for Malaya when the atom bombs were dropped. September 1945 saw her revisit Singapore for the first time since the events of February 1942. Other post-war duties included transporting Afrika Corps prisoners-of-war, remnants of Chandra Bose's rebel Indian National Army, displaced persons from Eastern Europe, and British troops to Palestine.

Derequisitioned in July 1948 after a major refit, she returned to the East Africa route. In 1953 she was sold to the British Iron and Steel Corporation for breaking up and returned to the United Kingdom at the end of May. She finally sailed into the Hughes, Bolckow yard at Blyth for dismantling. Frank Henderson of No. 4 OSC, who had been taken prisoner after disembarking at Singapore, went with John Nicholson, another ex-prisoner-of-war, to take a last look at her. It is

Durban 1942: A British Troopship Revolt

surely right that the final comments about the *City of Canterbury* should be left to one of those who sailed on her during her most dramatic moments:

> How memories came flooding back to us as we walked around the decks, through the dining rooms and cabins which, incidentally, we were seeing for the first time, as then we were common ORs. Our quarters had gone back to their original purpose – cargo holds. We took a few snaps of the ship and obtained a souvenir from the bathrooms. When we were moving off, we had a chat with the foreman in charge and he said that she was one of the cleanest ships they had ever had to break up.
>
> What a contrast to when we boarded her at Durban, where we all walked off in disgust at the filthy condition she was in. Remember, chaps![6]

Notes

Chapter 1

1. This is the date given in Frank C. Bowen, "Thirty-year Career of a 'City Boat'", *Sea Breezes*, 1953, p. 50, as, self-evidently, it is in J.H. Isherwood, "Ellerman Liner *City of Canterbury* of 1923", *Sea Breezes*, July 1978, pp. 418–20. However, the date 1922 appears both in Ministry of War Transport records (see infra) and in James Taylor, *Ellerman's: A Wealth of Shipping*, Wilton House Gentry, 1976 and in Duncan Haws, *Merchant Fleets: Ellerman Lines*, 1989 (the place of publication of books is London, unless otherwise indicated).
2. Ralph Barker, *Children of the Benares*, Methuen, 1987.
3. See note 1, above.
4. There have been a number of ships simply called the *Canterbury*. The captain of a mid eighteenth-century naval vessel of that name was found guilty of murder after killing the captain of HMS *Warwick* in a duel. See *The Trial of Capt. Edward Clark etc.* (1750). A much later HMS *Canterbury* was the "C" class light cruiser built by John Brown's of Clydebank in 1915. Perhaps the most memorable *Canterbury*, however, was the Southern Railway cross-channel ferry. Built at Dumbarton in 1928, she was scrapped in 1965, having seen wartime service at Calais, Dunkirk and Normandy. In his book *The Flames of Calais* (Grafton Books, 1989 reprint, pp. 67–71), Airey Neave suggested that the *City of Canterbury* transported the men of the Queen Victoria Rifles from Dover to Calais on May 22 1940 to hold up the German advance on Dunkirk. In fact, they sailed on the much smaller *Canterbury*. For details, see Public Record Office [PRO] MT59/1227, "Southern Railway Vessels and the War". Neave also added (pp. 92–3) that the *City of Canterbury* took the equipment of the King's Royal Rifle Corps from Southampton on May 22, arriving at Calais on the 23rd. This is *possible*, but frustratingly, the log of the *City of Canterbury* is blank for this period, and the *Sailings Book, 1933–1943* for the vessel similarly is silent for these crucial few days. Whether the *City of Canterbury* assisted at the Dunkirk evacuation between May 27 and June 4, 1940 is also unclear. According to the *Sailings Book*, she completed voyage No. 53 at Glasgow on May 15, and commenced voyage No. 54 (to South Africa and India) from the same port on June 1. After the *Herald of Free Enterprise* disaster in 1987 and the sale of Townsend Thoresen Ferries to the P&O Shipping Company, one of the *Free Enterprise* ferries was renamed the *Pride of Canterbury*. The third *City of Canterbury* (10,511 tons) built in 1964 at Barclay Curle shipyard, Glasgow, had originally been named *City of Adelaide*. Apart from the change of name to *City of*

Canterbury in 1973, she also sailed as *Cap Cleveland*, *Rubens* and *A.L. Pioneer* before being scrapped in 1983.

5. Ellerman's built a fourth *City of Canterbury* (7,691 tons) in 1976 in a German shipyard, Bremer Vulkan, Vegesack. She was sold out of service in 1981, and renamed *Arc Aeolos*. She was still in service in 1988.
6. C.B.A. Behrens, *Merchant Shipping and the Demands of War*, HMSO, 1955, p. 218. Betty Behrens (1904–1989) was a Cambridge historian and authority on eighteenth-century France and Prussia. Her husband was also an eminent historian, E.H. Carr. She worked in the Ministry of War Transport during the war.
7. *Ibid.*, p. 269.
8. *Ibid.*, pp. 270–1.
9. *Ibid.*, p. 273.
10. *Ibid.*, p. 275.
11. See Lt.-Col. H.F. Joslen, *Orders of Battle*, HMSO, 1960, ii, pp. 467, 482–3.
12. This and much of the subsequent information is taken from the report of the *City of Canterbury's* master to her owners, dated May 26 1942. A copy is among the City Line Ltd. papers held at Glasgow University.
13. See MT40/143 for her wartime voyages and specifications.
14. McGill diary, December 17 1940.
15. Information from C. Taylor, Edinburgh, who sailed in WS 5A aboard the Dutch vessel, *Costa Rica*.
16. McGill diary, January 5 1941.
17. Information from James F. Brown, Glasgow, radio officer on the *City of Derby* in convoy WS 5A.
18. Copies kindly supplied by Mrs. Muriel Butler, Milngavie, nr. Glasgow. Her late husband, Dugald Butler, was an engineer aboard the *City of Canterbury* between 1940 and 1942.
19. John Hall Spencer, *Battle of Crete*, White Lion Publishers, 1976, pp. 80–4.
20. *Ibid.*, p. 82.
21. Though the McGill diary refers to German markings on the attackers, they were probably Italian, as Hall Spencer suggests. Information also from J.R. Bradburn, Bury, one of the MNBDO marines on board the *City of Canterbury*.
22. James Leasor, *The Marine from Mandalay*, Leo Cooper, 1988, p. 8.
23. Hall Spencer, *Battle of Crete*, p. 83.
24. For a recent account, see Tony Simpson, *Operation Mercury: The Battle for Crete, 1941*, Hodder & Stoughton, 1981.

Notes

Chapter 2

1. Behrens, *Merchant Shipping and the Demands of War*, p. 250.
2. *Ibid.*, p. 256.
3. *Ibid.*, p. 257.
4. Copy in AIR 23/3582 (Overseas Command).
5. On Christmas Day 1941 Wavell also wired to General Sir Alan Brooke, the new Chief of the Imperial General Staff, "Am averse to withdrawing AA units from Iraq if avoidable. Understand some portion of WS 14 being transhipped to Durban. Request your decision *re* AA in WS 14 is reconsidered with view to both light and heavy regiments being sent to India." See ADM199/2234, East Indies War Diary (Naval), December 1–31 1941, p. 1002. TROOPERS (the Chiefs of Staff) could not oblige and the *City of Canterbury*, at least, benefited from the presence on board of gunners of the 48th Light AA Regt.
6. Major-General S. Woodburn Kirby, *The War against Japan*, i, *The Loss of Singapore*, HMSO, 1957, p. 259.
7. *Ibid.*, pp. 253–4.
8. The Hurricanes were being transported in convoy WS 12Z. The proposal from Far East command was that the convoy be diverted to Java where the planes would be assembled and then flown on to Singapore. See AIR 23/4711, "ABDAIR Air Reinforcements Policy, 27/8/41 – 21/2/42".
9. Kirby, *The War against Japan*, i, pp. 260–1.
10. *Ibid.*, p. 258.
11. AIR 23/3582
12. Kirby, *The War against Japan*, i, p. 258. For the embarkation orders of these AA regiments, see WO 166/2368 (77th HAA War Diary) and WO 166/2691 (21st LAA War Diary). They were in fact diverted to Batavia, the 77th arriving on the *Warwick Castle* in February. A day later, about 26 members of the regiment were killed in a train crash while being taken to barracks.
13. AIR 23/3582. It goes without saying that with the defeat in the Far East, company war diaries and RAF operations records books contain lengthy gaps. For 605 Squadron Operations Record Book, see AIR 27/2089. The last poignant entry before overseas service was dated October 31, 1941 and confided, "We now enthusiastically look forward to what November may bring". The next entry was RAF Ford, June 7 1942, stating tersely, "605 Squadron commenced to re-form. The squadron lost its identity when it proceeded overseas in the early part of the year. It is believed that most of the ground personnel were taken prisoner in Batavia." An interesting entry for June 14, 1942 announced that W/Cdr. P.W. Townsend DSO, DFC, had arrived to take command. Peter Townsend's autobiography suggests that his short stay at No. 605 Squadron was an unhappy one. See Peter Townsend, *Time and Chance: An Autobiography*, Collins, 1978, p. 117.

Durban 1942: A British Troopship Revolt

14. Another 48 pilots, plus 48 Hurricanes for these fighter squadrons, were being transported on the aircraft carrier *Indomitable*. See AIR 23/4711. In addition, ground personnel and equipment for No. 232 (Fighter) Squadron were in convoy WS 12Z, due to reach Singapore around January 9 1942, after being diverted.
15. AIR 23/3582.
16. Behrens, *Merchant Shipping*, Appendix XXXV.
17. Information from Jim McGeorge, Edinburgh, who sailed on the *Athlone Castle*.
18. ADM 199/1138.
19. Cited in Behrens, *Merchant Shipping*, p. 260.
20. *Ibid.*, p. 259.
21. MT 63/248, "Falla Report, March 3, 1942", for this and subsequent discussion.
22. Cited in Behrens, *Merchant Shipping*, p. 258.
23. ADM 199/2235. The Senior Sea Transport Officer at Durban had complained that on occasions when trans-shipment of cargoes was necessitated, sufficient advance details of cargo had not been received to arrange a stowage plan. See MT63/244, "Report of Visit to South African ports by Captain H. Vaughan-Jones, March 2, 1942."
24. AIR 23/3582.
25. MT 63/248.
26. *Ibid.*, C.W. Dixon (Assistant Under-Secretary of State, Dominions Office) to T.G. Jenkins (Deputy Director-General, Ministry of War Transport), November 7 1941.
27. *Ibid.*, Falla Report, p. 5.
28. The manager of the Union Castle agency, Mr. Hankinson, who had been acting for the MWT representative, was appointed Deputy. See MT 63/244. Vaughan-Jones' findings on behalf of the Director of Sea Transport, an Admiralty appointment, echoed many of the views of Brig. Falla. In particular, different persons should hold the posts of NLO and SSTO (i.e. PSTO) in Durban.
29. Behrens, *Merchant Shipping*, pp. 260–1.
30. See *Welcome to Durban*, wartime information leaflet distributed to troops in transit. Copy kindly supplied by Mr. T. Scollan, Droitwich Spa, Worcs.
31. For more detail of the social and welfare facilities in Durban available to merchant seamen, see MT 63/253, "Shipping in the Cape Route. Report to Minister of War Transport by C.E. Wurtzburg MC, and R.H. Tolerton CB, CBE, DSO, MC, on Completion of Mission, London, December 1942", paras. 99–104. Inevitably, separate seamen's institutes, according to colour, were recommended. Brigadier Falla, in his report, n. 21 above, also mentions this question.
32. Oliver Walker, "Convoy Blues", *Forum*, 4, No. 4, November 22 1941.
33. Pte. Alfred R. Evans, typescript narrative of war service, Imperial War Museum, 82/24/1.
34. LAC F.C. Welding, typescript narrative of war service, Imperial War Museum.
35. Captain E.A.S. Bailey, *SAWAS 1939–1947: Book of Thanks, 1980*, privately printed, p. 101.
36. Diary kindly supplied by John Ewan Preston of Kendal.
37. AIR 46/16, "British Air Ministry Liaison Mission, South Africa; Monthly Report for July 1942, Appendix I, p. 10".
38. WO 179/5857.
39. *Ibid.*, "Emergency Scheme".

Notes

Chapter 3

1. As well as holding the post of DJAG, W/Cdr. Shurlock was also a major, late of the Royal Engineers and Royal Fusiliers. He was formerly DJAG, British Forces, Middle East and DJAG, Allied Forces in France. A barrister (Lincoln's Inn), he was author of *Companies' Voluntary Liquidation*; *Company Prospectuses*; *Army Court-Martial Procedure*; *Royal Air Force Court-Martial Procedure*; *Army District Court-Martial Procedure and Notes on Field General Courts-Martial* (1941); and *600 Questions and Answers on Military Law*, 5th edition (1943).
2. Percival to City Line Ltd., voyage report, May 26 1942, pp. 9–10.
3. Information from A.P. Wheway, Seaford, East Sussex.
4. Percival to City Line, February 18 1942.
5. The STO was possibly Lt.-Cdr. Chesnutt, listed as STO II in Captain Vaughan-Jones' report of March 2 1942. See MT 63/244.
6. AIR 2/9204, Shurlock to JAG, March 16 1942 (hereafter Shurlock Report).
7. *Ibid.*, Frew to SNO, Simonstown, undated (probably January 16); Frew to Sir Philip Babington (Air Member for Personnel (AMP)), Air Ministry, January 16, 1942. References to subsequent signals are from AIR 2/9204 unless otherwise indicated.
8. *Ibid*. The signal was repeated to the GOC Malaya.
9. Available at General Register and Record Office of Shipping and Seamen, Cardiff.
10. AIR 2/9204, SNO, Simonstown to Admiralty, January 20 1942.
11. *Ibid.*, Donald to Babington, February 10 1942.
12. *Ibid.*, Salmon to Donald, February 6 1942.
13. Salisbury-Jones diary, January 14 1942 (Imperial War Museum).
14. AIR 2/9204, Salisbury-Jones to War Office, January 16 1942.
15. *Ibid*, MacGeagh to Babington, May 4 1942.
16. *Ibid.*, Fiddament to Babington, June 1 1942.
17. The Rulings Book was consulted with the kind permission of the then Judge Advocate General of the Forces, Mr. James Stuart-Smith C.B., Q.C.
18. War Office, *Manual of Military Law* (1914), pp. 39, 429–30, 631.
19. See note 16 above.
20. Most signals refer to 27 ORs, though the Shurlock Report mentions 29, which tallies with the notes kept by A.P. Wheway, who also calculates that 167 RAF personnel were left behind. It is possible that seven airmen had simply "missed the boat" or had deserted the ship independently of the protest. Naval vessels arriving in South Africa often had experience of sailing without their full complement after a stay in Cape Town or Durban. This happened to the *Prince of Wales* after docking at Cape Town, en route to Singapore. See Martin Middlebrook and Patrick Mahoney, *Battleship*, Penguin Books, 1979, p. 69.
21. According to Hugh Preston's diary entry for February 7 1942, the sergeant was found guilty of *inciting* mutiny.

Durban 1942: A British Troopship Revolt

22. In 1957, the Court-Martial Appeal Court went further and drew a distinction between collective disobedience which was not a mutiny, and collective insubordination, defiance or disregard of authority, which was. See *R* v. *Grant* [1957] 1 W.L.R. 906. Disobeying one single order without repudiating military or air force authority would not then appear to constitute mutiny. But if the single order is to march to the "Front" (or even to board a troopship?), a different conclusion is surely tenable.
23. See note 15 above.
24. Shurlock Report.
25. AIR 2/9204, Babington to Donald, June 8 1942.
26. *Ibid.*, Babington to Secretary of State, July 8 1942. For another view of the fate of the Army personnel, see below, Chapter Four.

Chapter 4

1. Vague recollections of an Army Fire Fighting Unit and even an Army Carrier Pigeon Unit on board have been expressed to the author. There is no independent corroboration.
2. The sources relied upon are, principally, the written or verbal narratives of the participants and the "Statements of Evidence" to the courts-martial, submitted by various Service staffs serving in Durban who were directly involved in dealing with the protesters. Copies of the latter kindly supplied by John Ewan Preston, Kendal, and Terence Billing, Norwich.
3. The morning inspection team also included Captain Williams, Embarkation Medical Officer.
4. "Statements of Evidence: Major Albert Edmund Neville Clarke".
5. A. Babington, *For the Sake of Example: Capital Courts-Martial, 1914–1919*, Leo Cooper, 1983.
6. For the exceptional case of the Cocos-Keeling Islands executions in 1942, see below, Chapter Seven.
7. This may well have been Captain E.S. Henochsberg KC of the Union Defence Forces, who had been supplied as judge advocate by Col. J.A. Watermeyer, Chief of the UDF Legal Department. Captain Maisels was also appointed to assist as judge advocate. See AIR 2/9204, Shurlock Report.
8. For this, and subsequent details of convoy WS 15, see ADM 199/1211 and ADM 237/268.
9. Information from C. Powell, Stockport, with RAF senior NCOs escorting POWs on the *Orbita*. The *Orbita* herself was scarcely a model of salubrity. In 1946 Australian troops set fire to her in protest at her condition. When the family of the submariner, Cdr. Alastair Mars, sailed on her to join him on service in New Zealand, Mrs. Mars was required by the Ministry of Transport to sign a paper promising that she would not complain about the accommodation. See Alastair Mars, *Court Martial*, Frederick Muller Ltd., 1954, p. 87.
10. This is the view of Terence Billing.

Notes

Chapter 5

1. AIR 2/9204, Fiddament to Babington, June 1 1942.
2. *Ibid.*, Babington to Secretary of State, July 8 1942. For "Far East", we should, of course, read "India".
3. *Ibid.*, Air Directorate, South African Air Force, to Under Secretary of State, Air Ministry (London), October 27 1942.
4. *Ibid.*, Air Ministry to Frew, July 21 1942.
5. See note 1, above.
6. *Ibid.*, DPS to AO i/c Records, Gloucester, November 8 1945.
7. *Ibid.*, AOC No. 18 Group to Under Secretary of State, January 25 1951; *ibid.*, DPS to AOC No. 18 Group, February 2 1951.
8. *Ibid.*, L.M. Hooper to "The Superior Air Force Authority", February 14 1942.
9. See note 2, above.
10. *Ibid.*, Frew to Under Secretary of State, April 14 1942 (probably the Permanent Under-Secretary (PUS), Sir Arthur Street).
11. *Ibid.*, Air Ministry to Frew, April 6 1942.
12. *Ibid.*, Frew to Air Ministry, April 15 1942.
13. *Ibid.*, Air Ministry to Frew, April 21 1942.
14. See note 2, above.
15. *Ibid.*, Secretary of State to Babington, July 10 1942.
16. See note 10, above.
17. See note 11, above.
18. AIR 46/16.
19. AIR 2/9204, Jasper to Director of Movements, August 13 1942.
20. *Ibid.*, Sims to Jasper, August 14 1942; Jasper to Sims, August 18 1942.
21. *Ibid.*, September 28 1942.
22. *Ibid.*, Sims to DPS, November 24 1942.
23. The division of responsibility on the quayside between the embarkation officer and the assistant provost-marshal (i.e. once the troopship had sailed without the mutineers) does not seem to have been resolved.
24. AIR 2/9204, Section 10(a) to H.R. Ould (a principal in the Department of the PUS), DPS and Dir. Movements, December 24 1942.
25. *Ibid.*, Jasper to D. Movements, September 1 1943.
26. *Ibid.*, Sims to Central Registry, Secret Section, January 10 1945.
27. *Ibid.*, DPS to JAG, May 30 1945.

Durban 1942: A British Troopship Revolt

Chapter 6

1. DO 35/1632, "Harlech Report, March 1943".
2. *Forum*, 4, February 7 1942, p. 9.
3. *Natal Mercury*, January 23 1942.
4. *Ibid.*, February 3, 9 1942. For an instance in the UK when a *Daily Express* journalist was found guilty of breaching Defence Regulations on censorship by reporting warship movements to his newspaper on an open telephone line, see ADM 1/15863, "Press Reporters: Censorship of Reports to Editors, 1944".
5. ADM 199/1211, "WS Convoys: WS 15".
6. DO 119/1151, Sir E.J. Harding to Lord Harlech, December 31 1942.
7. ADM 199/1276 for this and subsequent information.
8. Salisbury-Jones' personal war diary, his typescript autobiography, *My Friends, the French: Memoirs of a British St. Cyrien*, and various assorted papers are in the Imperial War Museum. They cast little light on this phase of his career, save to underline his unhappiness with his South African posting and his admiration for Smuts. According to his diary entry for January 14 1942, Salisbury-Jones, on hearing of the Durban protest, had proposed that the NCOs be court-martialled and the rest be dealt with summarily. This, of course, did not happen in the case of the RAF men but remains a possibility (until further evidence is forthcoming) in respect to the Army personnel. For Salisbury-Jones' activities at No. 27 British Military Mission in Greece in early 1941, see Robin Higham, *Diary of a Disaster: British Aid to Greece, 1940–1941*, University Press of Kentucky, Lexington, 1986, pp. 110–13.
9. Ellis to Salisbury-Jones, February 10 1942 (copy in *Natal Mercury* archives). On February 4 1942, Ellis attended a meeting at the Bureau of Information to discuss a proposed "Don't Chatter" campaign. The Director of Information was A.N. Wilson. See ADM 199/653, "South Atlantic: War Diaries".
10. DO 119/1151, Harding to Harlech, October 30, November 13 1942.
11. Ellis to Salisbury-Jones, February 10 1942.
12. DO 119/1150, Harding to Harlech, supplement to letter 11/42 (not in file), *c.* June 25 1942.
13. Ellis to Salisbury-Jones, February 10 1942.
14. Salisbury-Jones to Ellis, February 17 1942.
15. AIR 2/9204, Harlech to Air Commodore Frew, February 3 1942.
16. Ellis to Salisbury-Jones, February 10 1942.
17. See the decision of the Independent Broadcasting Authority to transmit the programme, *Death on the Rock*, about the Gibraltar SAS shootings in 1988.
18. See note 15, above.
19. *Ibid.*, Frew to Harlech, February 9 1942. Frew nonetheless later wrote to the Air Ministry in April 1942, pointing out that since the RAF in South Africa was "attached" to the Union Defence Forces, an arrangement which apparently accorded with "local feeling", it was necessary for the RAF to create "the rather artificial devices" (i.e. RAF Unit No. 2, Clairwood Camp) to secure RAF autonomy. This presumably was a source of resentment among some of the local, informed population. See *ibid.*, Frew to Under-Secretary of State, Air Ministry, April 14 1942.
20. *Ibid.*, Harlech to Frew, February 14 1942.
21. Salisbury-Jones, *My Friends, the French*, p. 248.

Notes

22. E.A.Walker, *South Africa* (Oxford Pamphlets on World Affairs, No. 39), 1940, pp. 20–3.
23. See George Cloete Visser, *OB: Traitors or Patriots*, Macmillan, Cape Town, 1976.
24. DO 35/588/G91/419, Harlech to Cranborne, Dominions Office, October 23 1941. The plight of "poor whites" was not apparent to Harlech when he wrote to Paul Emrys-Evans who was taking over as minister in the Dominions Office in March 1942. Since the fall of Singapore, Harlech wrote, the problems of accommodating all the refugees were acute, "where the standards of living of the whites are so fantastically high in a country where there are 2 million white aristocrats and 8.5 million Coloureds, Indians and Natives! And where such things as rent control, price control, compulsory billeting etc. are either non-existent or 'pour rire'." Emrys-Evans MSS, Brit. Lib., Add. MSS 58244, ff. 1–2. Harlech to Emrys-Evans, March 5 1942.
25. Even among the black population of South Africa, 80,000 of whom enlisted in the SADF, a quarter of its complement, attitudes were complex. Some refused to join the Army on the ground that, "it was a white man's war and did not concern them". For a full analysis, see Louis Grundlingh, "The Recruitment of South African Blacks for Participation in the Second World War", in David Killingray and Richard Rathbone (eds.), *Africa and the Second World War*, Macmillan, 1986, at p. 193.
26. Walker, *South Africa*, p. 32.
27. DO 35/1632.
28. *Ibid*.

Durban 1942: A British Troopship Revolt

Chapter 7

1. Lawrence James, *Mutiny in the British and Commonwealth Forces, 1797–1956*, Buchan & Enright, 1987.
2. *Ibid.*, p. 13.
3. Whether the Judge Advocate General held an advisory or a judicial post was a matter of dispute in the nineteenth century. It may be argued that the position is still not wholly free from doubt at the theoretical level. But currently the Courts-Martial Appeal Court is required by statute to have regard to any expression of opinion by the JAG in considering whether a case is a fit one for appeal. In 1956 the Lord Chancellor advised informally that a "Ruling" of the JAG, "should be treated with the respect that a civil court of first instance would, by the practice of comity between the courts, accord to a decision of another court of its own standing". See prefatory note to JAG's *Rulings Book* in series WO 210.
4. Dudley Pope, *The Devil Himself: The Mutiny of 1800*, Alison Press/Secker & Warburg, 1987.
5. WO 32/15243; *Report of the Select Committee on the Army and Air Force Acts*, P.P. 1952–53 (289) iii, 629, Appendix B; James, *Mutiny*, pp. 229–32.
6. *Ibid.* An eighth man was tried at Singapore in 1948. His death sentence, on conviction, was also commuted to penal servitude for life.
7. For the Indian National Army, see James, *Mutiny*, pp. 235–7. For the Indian Liberation Army, see Anna Bramwell, letter to *Independent Magazine*, May 20 1989.
8. Andrew Rothstein, *The Soldiers' Strikes of 1919*, Journeyman Press, 1980. Shortly after the conclusion of the Second World War, British merchant seamen refused to crew the *Moreton Bay*, taking 1,000 Dutch conscripts to the Dutch East Indies to fight the Indonesian Liberation Army. The conscripts had been transferred from the *Stirling Castle*, whose crew had also refused to sail. See Richard Kisch, *The Days of the Good Soldiers: Communists in the Armed Forces, WWII*, Journeyman Press, 1985, p. 119. According to one author, British soldiers opposed to the restoration of British colonial rule in Malaya gave the Malayan Communists, who had, of course, been allies in the anti-Japanese guerrilla war, advance warning of attacks being planned against them by the British Army. See Peter Tatchell, *Democratic Defence: A Non-Nuclear Alternative*, GMP Publishers Ltd., 1985, pp. 170–1.
9. For the Connaught Rangers Mutiny, see James, *Mutiny*, pp. 202–8; WO 32/4235. For the Curragh Incident, see Ian F.W. Beckett (ed.), *The Army and the Curragh Incident*, Army Records Society, ii, Bodley Head, 1986; I.F.W. Beckett and Keith Jeffery, "The Royal Navy and the Curragh Incident," *Historical Research*, 62, February 1989, pp. 54–69.
10. Alan Patient, "Mutiny at Salerno", *Listener*, February 25 1982, pp. 8–9; Nico Keijzer, *Military Obedience*, Sijthoff & Noordhoff, Amsterdam, 1978, pp. 57–8; WO 32/15243; P.P. 1952–53 (289), iii, 629, Appendix B; James, *Mutiny*, pp. 171–3.
11. The following examples, unless otherwise indicated, are taken from the last three sources in note 10, above.

Notes

12. Sections 8 and 9, covering striking or threatening a superior officer and disobedience to a superior officer, were to be charged in cases of insubordination, even on the part of two or more, if there did not appear to be a combined design to resist authority.
13. Bill Glenton, *Mutiny In Force X*, Hodder & Stoughton, 1986, for this and subsequent references.
14. The renamed vessel is listed as an auxiliary cruiser during her war service. She was built in 1938 by Cammell Laird, Birkenhead, and returned to the City Line in 1946. In 1961 she was sold to the Hong Kong Salvage Towing Company, renamed the *Castle Mount*, and broken up in Hong Kong in the same year. See Taylor, *Ellerman's: A Wealth of Shipping*, p. 263.
15. Ken Stofer, "Mutiny in the R.A.F., or All Aboard the Woodlark", *Fighting Forces*, 3, June/July 1989, pp. 57–8.
16. Information from E. Sellick, Exeter and V. Davidson, Manchester.
17. L.E. Ransom, war narrative, Imperial War Museum, 87/42/1, p. 7.
18. DO 119/1150, Harding to Harlech, July 3 1942.
19. A.K. Berrecloth, war narrative, Imperial War Museum, PP/MCR/297, p. 87.
20. See note 8, above.
21. Its proceedings featured in June 1989 in the BBC 2 drama series, *Vote for Them*. See also Bill Davidson, "The Cairo Forces Parliament", *Labour History Review*, 55, Part 3, 1990, pp. 20–6. Sergeant Davidson was the "Foreign Secretary" in the Parliament and later advised the BBC on the production of the television series. He died on November 9 1989.
22. See also Basil Davidson, *Special Operations Europe: Scenes from the Anti-Nazi War*, Grafton Books, 1987, pp. 203–8.
23. Penelope Summerfield, "Education and Politics in the British Armed Forces in the Second World War", *International Review of Social History*, 26, 1981, pp. 133–58.
24. See, for example, *British Soldier in India: The Letters of Clive Branson*, The Communist Party, 1944. At a mass meeting in early 1945 aboard the *Andes* (from which, it will be recalled, many of the RAF personnel transferred in 1942 to the *City of Canterbury*), "over 500 soldiers voted overwhelmingly in favour of immediate independence for India". See Tatchell, *Democratic Defence*, p. 170. See, also, John Prance, letter to the *Guardian*, September 19 1986.
25. Tatchell, *Democratic Defence*, p. 167. The author adds, "Far from being ready to move against the election of a radical socialist government, a small section of the army contemplated a military coup against the Tories if Churchill was re-elected. They even went so far as to discuss the possibility of asking Field-Marshal Montgomery to head a military-backed anti-Tory government." See *ibid*. The authority for this claim is not given. According to Summerfield, "Education and Politics", p. 133, 64 per cent of all servicemen signed a Service Register in November 1944 and 37 per cent actually voted in July 1945. The author adds that the soldiers' votes made little difference to the outcome.
26. Tony Mason, "Soldiers, War and Politics", summary of seminar paper, Warwick University, October 1988.
27. Richard Sibley, "The Swing to Labour During the Second World War: When and Why", *Labour History Review*, 55, Part 1, 1990, pp. 23–29.

28. See note 18, above.
29. While some of the Durban mutineers, as we have seen, ended up at the maintenance depot at RAF Drigh Road, Karachi, none of those contacted were there at the time of the mass-mutiny of RAF personnel in India and the Far East in early 1946. That famous mutiny was caused by delays in demobilisation. See Kisch, *The Days of the Good Soldiers*, Chapters Nine and Ten; Bernard Shilling, "Mutiny!", *Aeroplane Monthly*, December 1986, pp. 660–1. For mutinies among African troops over slow demobilisation, see David Killingray and Richard Rathbone, "Introduction", in Killingray and Rathbone (eds.), *Africa and the Second World War*, p. 15. Occasional incidents of collective disobedience surfaced from time to time after the war. See the typical "Cases of Mutiny Received in Judge Advocate General's Office, September 1 1948 to August 31 1949", P.P. 1952–53 (289), iii, *op. cit.*, Appendix C, 1131–2; WO 32/15243; James, *Mutiny*, p. 177. An unpublished incident in mid 1946 concerned the refusal of officers and men of an RAF ground crew at a Staging Post in Kano, Nigeria, to service civilian aircraft of the Nigerian Posts and Telegraph Office (NPTO) using the RAF station. The cause of the refusal, which shut down the Staging Post, was the repeated non-arrival of the men's letters and parcels from home, which would not be loaded on board the Dakotas if the planes were full with bags from the NPTO. After four days the complaint was finally rectified. No recriminations followed this incident, though an air vice-marshal (possibly G.J. Salmon) visited the Post to investigate the matter three weeks later. Information from Desmond ("Don") Palmer, Canterbury. One might hazard the guess that such small-scale incidents were not uncommon in the Armed Forces in the post-war years.

Notes

Chapter 8

1. For the escape route via Padang, see Richard Gough, *The Escape from Singapore*, William Kimber, 1987, chapters 8 and 9. For Lyon's exploits, see Brian Connell, *Return of the Tiger*, Sundial Publications, 1980. They featured on a recent television series entitled *Heroes*.
2. See for example the table in Denis Russell-Roberts, *Spotlight on Singapore*, Douglas, Isle of Man: Times Press, 1965, pp. 184–5; Gough, *The Escape from Singapore*, Appendix 1; and David Nelson, *The Story of Changi*, Changi Publication Co., Australia, 1974, Appendix B.
3. Lord Russell of Liverpool, *The Knights of Bushido*, Corgi Books, 1980 reprint. Russell was Deputy Judge Advocate General whose Office prepared war crimes cases for prosecution.
4. ADM 1/14341 for this and subsequent information. Cf. Geoffrey Brooke, *Alarm Starboard!*, Patrick Stephens, Cambridge, 1982, p. 273.
5. Russell of Liverpool, *The Knights of Bushido*, p. 56.
6. FEPOW *Forum*, Christmas 1953. The author is indebted to Edward McDaniel for this reference.

Index

Air Council 47-8, 75, 79-80
Air Ministry 37, 41, 46, 49, 51, 53, 79, 81, 83, 86, 89
—, Liaison Mission, Pretoria 32-3, 37
Allied Prisoners of War 124-7, 131
Army Units:
—, British:
—, —, Connaught Rangers 108
—, —, 9th Division 21
—, —, 11th Division 21
—, —, 18th Division 20, 23, 123
—, —, 46th Division 108
—, —, 50th Division 108
—, —, 51st (Highland) Division 108
—, —, 234th HAA Battery 15-16
—, —, 60th HAA Regiment 6
—, —, 68th HAA Regiment 10, 13, 15
—, —, 77th HAA Regiment 22, 131
—, —, 89th HAA Regiment 6
—, —, King's Royal Rifle Corps 129
—, —, 21st LAA Regiment 22, 131
—, —, 101st LAA Regiment 31
—, —, No. 4 OSC, RAOC 22, 56-8, 64, 77, 124, 126-7
—, —, Queen Victoria Rifles 129
—, Imperial:
—, —, 8th (Australian) Division 21
—, —, Ceylon Defence Force 107
—, —, 7th Gold Coast Regiment 107
—, —, 44th Indian Infantry Brigade Group 21
—, —, 1st Battalion, Mauritius Regiment 110
—, —, 1st South African Division 102-3
—, —, Witwatersrand Rifles 66
Assistant Provost-Marshal 45, 81, 136
Atkinson, Captain T.K.W. 125
Attlee, Clement 91
Australian Servicemen 15, 17, 30, 56, 63, 65, 125
—, and Deserters 125-6

Babington, Sir Philip 46-7, 52, 79
Batavia (see also under 'Ports') 77, 123-6, 131
Behrens, C.A.B. 3, 19, 24, 27, 130
Biddle, Flight Lieutenant L.J. 72-5
Bradley, Flight Lieutenant D. 44-5, 74, 81
Budgen, Rear-Admiral D.A. 91-2

Campbell, A.M. 26, 28
Canadian Sergeant-Pilots 56, 115
Canterbury Tales 11
Censorship 11, 91-9, 137
Chiefs of Staff 4, 20-3, 25, 131
City of Canterbury (pre-1875) 2
—, (built 1875) 2
—, (built 1964) 129
—, (built 1976) 130
—, (built 1923):
—, —, April 1942 walk-off 114-5
—, —, attack en route to Suda Bay 14-15
—, —, at Batavia 125
—, —, breaking up 127-8
—, —, at Calais 129
—, —, career after February 1942 127-8
—, —, conditions on board 10-13, 38-44, 56-9, 61-3, 123, 128
—, —, and convoy WS 5A 3, 5-9
—, —, crew members 42, 130
—, —, disturbance aboard, April 1941 11-13
—, —, at Durban 35
—, —, Durban walk-off, 37-44, 57-66, 106, 128
—, —, in the Middle East 10, 17
—, —, pre-war career 1-3
—, —, sails to Far East 66
—, —, at Singapore 124
—, —, at Suda Bay 15-16
—, —, voyage routes 2-3
Clairwood Transit Camp 29, 32-5, 40, 66, 71, 83, 85, 96, 100, 113-4, 117

Durban 1942: A British Troopship Revolt

Clark, Major A.E.N. 66, 82, 85
Convoys:
—, BM12 21, 123
—, CM 5
—, DM2 21, 123
—, in general 3-5, 19, 21, 97, 114
—, WS 5A 3, 5-9, 130
—, WS 12Z 131
—, WS 14 4, 21-2, 37-8, 113, 131
—, WS 15 53, 76, 79
Court Martial:
—, disposal of offenders after 53, 75-7, 79
—, proceedings and sentences 51-3, 71-5, 79, 95-8, 100, 103, 107-10, 116, 122, 138
—, proposals to conduct 45-51, 136
—, statutes 119

Death Penalty 50, 72, 107-10, 120, 138
Donald, Air Vice-Marshal Grahame 44
Durban:
—, in general 9, 13, 23-4, 28-32, 67, 69-70, 132
—, other shipboard disturbances in 113-5
Dutch East Indies (Java and Sumatra) 21, 125-6, 131

Ellis, Mervyn 95-103
Emrys-Evans, Paul 136
Erskine, Squadron-Leader T.J. 42-3, 50-1, 64-7, 73, 81, 83-4, 87-9

Falla, Brigadier N.S. 25-7, 85, 132
Fiddament, Air Commodore Arthur 47-8, 50, 79-80
Forces' Parliament 119, 121, 139
Frew, Air Commodore M.B. 33, 39-42, 47, 55, 63-4, 82-5, 99-100, 136

Gibson, Perla 9, 30-1
Glenton, Bill 110, 112-3
Goldsmith, Colonel C.T. 41, 45

Hankinson, Mr. 28, 132
Harding, Sir E.J. 95, 97, 122
Harlech, Lord 24-6, 75, 91, 95, 98-100, 102-3, 122, 136
Hertzog, J.B.M. 101
Hetherington, R.W.J. 1, 18, 42, 124, 127
Hooper, Wing Commander L.M. 51, 73, 81
Hopkinson, Captain E.H. 92

Imperial Air Force Units:
—, No. 1, Aerodrome Construction Unit (Unit 24), RNZAF 124-5
—, No. 413 (RCAF) Squadron 115
—, No. 453 (Australian) Squadron 125
Imperial Movement Control 27, 66, 82, 85
Indian Liberation Army 108
Indian National Army 108, 127
Indiscipline and Insubordination 10, 105, 107, 117, 140
Indonesian Liberation Army 139
Italian Prisoners of War 10, 17-18, 37-8, 57, 70, 114

James, Lawrence 105
Japanese Attacks 19-20, 38, 59, 79, 123, 125
Jasper, G.C. 86-8
Judge Advocate General (see also 'MacGeagh, Sir Harry') 106, 134, 139, 140

Kercher, Wing Commander 38, 43, 61, 87-9

Law:
—, Air Force 46-53, 73, 81, 86-90, 106, 139
—, Military 48-53, 81, 106-7, 121, 139
Lawrence, Harry 95
Longstaff, Captain Ralph 127

MacGeagh, Sir Harry 39, 47-9, 51-3, 88-9
McGill, T. 6, 16-17, 130
Malan, D.F. 101, 103
Malaya 20-1, 56, 127
Malayan Communists 139
Ministry of War Transport 3-4, 24-5, 85
Mobile Naval Base Defence Organization 14-15, 17, 130
Muggeridge, Malcolm 92
'Mutineers':
—, A—, J. 81
—, Billing, Terence 59, 61, 77
—, Carter, Ron 60-1, 63, 66, 68, 72, 75-7
—, Docherty, William 66, 77
—, E—, John 69, 74
—, Fishwick, Joe 58, 62, 65, 77, 80
—, K—, Norman 76
—, McK—, F. 80
—, Peacock, David 68, 73-4, 77
—, Preston, Hugh 31, 58, 62, 70-7
—, Sharp, David 58, 60, 62-3, 74, 77
—, Smith, D.C.G. 68, 71, 73, 75, 79-80
—, Welding, F.C. 30, 59, 62, 64-6, 68-70, 73-6, 132

144

Index

Mutiny:
—, in general 1, 50-1, 64, 73, 105, 133
—, specific instances and walk-offs:
—, —, African troops 140
—, —, *Bounty* 105, 107
—, —, Christmas Island 107-8
—, —, Cocos-Keeling Islands 107
—, —, Connaught Rangers 108
—, —, Curragh Incident 108
—, —, *Ellenga* 115-16
—, —, Force X 110-13
—, —, Italy, 1944 110
—, —, Kano 140
—, —, Madagascar 110
—, —, Mersa Matruh 109
—, —, *Moreton Bay* 138
—, —, Napoleonic Wars 107
—, —, North Africa rail journey 109-10
—, —, RAF in India and Far East, 1946 140
—, —, Salerno 108-9
—, Statistics 120

Nash, Captain 40
Neave, Airey 129
New Zealand Servicemen 15, 17, 124-5
No. 203 U.K. Military Liaison Mission, Pretoria 33, 41, 46, 94

Osmond, W.R.F. 89

Paine, Les 126
Peaty, Major Robert 22, 57, 82, 87-8
Percival, Captain Herbert 6-9, 11-12, 14, 16, 18, 38-42, 64, 124, 127
Pirow, Oswald 102-3
Politics and the Armed Forces (see also 'Forces' Parliament') 117-19, 121-2, 139
Port Health Authority, Durban (also Port Health Officer) 42-3
Ports (see also 'Durban', and '*City of Canterbury*: Voyage Routes')
—, Aden 17-18, 37, 76
—, Alexandria 5, 13-14, 17, 27, 30
—, Avonmouth 57
—, Balboa 111
—, Batavia (Tandjong Priok) 21, 23, 125-6
—, Berbera 18
—, Blyth 127
—, Bombay 19, 76, 114-15, 127
—, Brest 8
—, Calais 129
—, Calcutta 19, 27
—, Cape Town 10, 23, 25, 45, 77, 91, 93, 117, 122, 134
—, Colombo 10, 19, 115, 125-7
—, Dover 129
—, East London 24
—, Freetown 9, 23
—, Glasgow 6, 127, 129
—, Halifax 10
—, Horta 76
—, Karachi 115
—, Liverpool 7, 77
—, Lourenço Marques 92
—, Madras 115-16
—, Mombasa 18, 63
—, Naples 127
—, New York 111-12
—, Oosthaven 21
—, Pearl Harbor 23-4, 34
—, Port Elizabeth 24
—, Port Said 13, 17
—, Port Suez (Suez Bay) 5, 15, 17-18
—, Port T (Addu Attol) 76-7
—, Port Tewfik 9, 31
—, Simonstown 24, 37, 43, 91
—, Singapore (Keppel Harbour) 19, 21-3, 38, 123-4
—, Southampton 127, 129
—, Sydney 21
—, Takoradi 7
—, Tjilatjap 123-5
—, Trincomalee 113
Pote, Doryn 31, 64

Reinforcements 20, 22-3, 25, 56, 131
Royal Air Force Units:
—, No. 24 Air Sea Rescue Main Craft Unit 80-1
—, No. 41 Air Stores Park 22
—, No. 2 Detachment, Durban 47-8, 136
—, No. 47, Embarkation Office 22
—, No. 18 Group 81
—, No. 151 Maintenance Unit 124-5
—, No. 301 Maintenance Unit 77, 115, 126
—, No. 21 Operations Room, Chittagong 77
—, No. 62 Repair and Salvage Unit 22
—, No. 5 Squadron 77
—, No. 22 Squadron 115
—, No. 191 Squadron 77
—, No. 240 Squadron 77
—, No. 146 (F) Squadron 77
—, No. 232 (F) Squadron 131
—, No. 242 (F) Squadron 22
—, No. 258 (F) Squadron 22
—, No. 605 (F) Squadron 22, 131

—, No. 266 Wing Headquarters 22
—, Bases:
—, —, Ambala, Northern India 76
—, —, Asanol, West Bengal 77
—, —, Bangalore, Southern India 76
—, —, Calshot 75
—, —, Colerne 81
—, —, Cox's Bazaar, East Bengal 77
—, —, Dinjan, Assam 76-7
—, —, Durban Pool 51-2
—, —, Jessore, East Bengal 77
Russel of Liverpool, Lord 140

Salisbury-Jones, Brigadier A.G. 33, 45, 95-6, 98, 100-1, 136
Salmon, Wing Commander C.J. 44
SAWAS and *SAWAS Book of Thanks* 3, 31, 76, 132
Schofield, B.M. 94
Sea Transport Officer (also Assistant, Divisional, Principal and Senior Sea Transport Officer) 15, 24, 27, 38, 40-1, 43, 60-1, 65, 81, 83, 85, 131-3
Servicemen (see also 'Mutineers' and under individual names):
—, Officers:
—, —, Annesley, Captain J.C. 93
—, —, Black, Captain 39
—, —, Brooke, General Sir Alan 131
—, —, Chrystal, Brigadier Jack 121
—, —, Daniel, Brigadier 39, 100
—, —, Ferguson, Colonel Alan 124
—, —, Fox, Captain 93
—, —, Gordon-Brown, Pilot Officer R.S. 67, 116-17
—, —, Havers, Sub-Lieutenant John 15-16
—, —, Henochsberg, Captain E.S. 134
—, —, Johnston, Flight Lieutenant L.M. 83
—, —, Joliffe, Flight Lieutenant 38
—, —, Layton, Admiral Sir Geoffrey 20
—, —, Lyon, Major Ivan, 124, 140
—, —, Maisels, Captain 134
—, —, Mars, Commander Alastair 134
—, —, Maund, Captain 92
—, —, May, Captain 93
—, —, Petrie, Captain 111
—, —, Pownall, Lieutenant-General Sir Henry 20
—, —, Redgrove, Squadron-Leader A.L. 83-4
—, —, Skaife, Major 122
—, —, Steward, Major Cuthbert 67

—, —, Stewart, Major H. 67
—, —, Tait, Vice-Admiral C. 93, 95-6
—, —, Tottenham, Admiral 94
—, —, Watermayer, Colonel J.A. 134
—, —, Wavell, General 20
—, —, Webster, Colonel William 94
—, —, Williams, Captain 134
—, —, Yates, Captain Henry 67
—, Others:
—, —, Adam, Sergeant Walter 59, 64
—, —, Andrews, Flight Sergeant 38
—, —, Arnott, John 16
—, —, Batchelor, William 58, 125-6
—, —, Berrecloth, Ken 117-18
—, —, Bourne, W.J. 126
—, —, Bradburn, J.R. 130
—, —, Brett, L.S. 11
—, —, Brinton, Warrant Officer 38
—, —, Carboni, Corporal Ernest 33
—, —, Clark, W.F. 126
—, —, Clarke, J.L. 12
—, —, Clayton, Pay-Sergeant Ron 57, 124, 126
—, —, Davidson, Sergeant Bill 139
—, —, Dobinett, Regimental Sergeant-Major 6
—, —, Dunn, Leonard 12
—, —, Evans, Alfred 29, 57, 132
—, —, Farringdon, Ron 58, 60-1, 66
—, —, Finch, Bernard 125-6
—, —, Gower, T.E. 113-14
—, —, Griffiths, L.J. 126
—, —, Hanson, Staff-Sergeant Doug. 57, 60
—, —, Hastain, Sub-Conductor Ron 57
—, —, Henderson, Frank 127-8
—, —, Hill, E.W. 17
—, —, Kinnear, William 56-7, 64
—, —, Knight, Edwin, 59, 61-2, 64
—, —, Lawrence, Ken 32
—, —, Lenzi, Corporal J. 62-3
—, —, McCarthy, Aircraftman 38
—, —, McDaniel, Edward 59, 63
—, —, McGeorge, Jim 58, 60, 63, 131
—, —, Maxwell, John B. 31
—, —, Merrett, James 114
—, —, Morrison, Joe 56
—, —, Nevin, John 58, 66, 126
—, —, Nicholson, John 127
—, —, Parish, Wilfred 127
—, —, Paterson, George 66, 126
—, —, Peterson, L. 30
—, —, Powell, C. 134
—, —, Pressley, Private 63

Index

—, —, Ralph, Leonard 126
—, —, Ransom, Corporal L.E. 115-16
—, —, Reason, Corporal Sidney 67
—, —, Scollan, T. 32-1, 132
—, —, Smith, J.C. 60
—, —, Steele, Arthur 15
—, —, Thomas, Gordon 32
—, —, Townsend, Gerald 29
—, —, True, Regimental Sergeant-Major 57, 126
—, —, Walmsley, G. 58
—, —, Watts, George 65
—, —, Wheeler, A.E. 32
—, —, Wheway, A.P. 38, 56, 118, 133
Shenton, Wing Commander R.F. 47-9
Ships (see also *City of Canterbury*):
—, Royal Navy:
—, —, *Abdiel* 17
—, —, *Argus* 6-7
—, —, *Ark Royal* 92
—, —, *Atreus* 9
—, —, *Berwick* 7-8
—, —, *Bonaventure* 6-7
—, —, *Bridgewater* 23
—, —, *Canterbury* 129
—, —, *Cornwall* 11
—, —, *Danae* (in Napoleonic Wars) 107
—, —, *Danae* 56-7, 107
—, —, *Derbyshire* 23
—, —, *Durban* 125
—, —, *Exeter* 123
—, —, *Flamingo* 14
—, —, *Formidable* 7, 9
—, —, *Furious* 6-7
—, —, *Glasgow* 11
—, —, *Hecla* 93
—, —, *Illustrious* 9
—, —, *Kedah* 125
—, —, *Lothian* 110-13
—, —, *Maidstone* 57
—, —, *Phoebe* 11
—, —, *Prince of Wales* 133
—, —, *Ramillies* 23, 77
—, —, *Shropshire* 9
—, —, *Worcestershire* 92
—, —, *York* 16
—, Other Navies:
—, —, *Admiral Hipper* (German) 8-9
—, —, *Borden* (German) 8
—, —, *Dipavati* (Indian) 76
—, —, *Lawrence* (Indian) 76
—, —, *Sutlej* (Indian) 124
—, —, *Waterhen* (Australian) 17
—, Merchant and Passenger:

—, —, *Adviser* 6
—, —, *Andes* 22-3, 29, 57, 71, 113
—, —, *Anselm* 7, 10
—, —, *Arabistan* 6, 8
—, —, *Arranbank* 16
—, —, *Athlone Castle* 22, 56, 75-6, 131
—, —, *Barrister* 6
—, —, *Benvinnes* 6
—, —, *Bhutan* 7
—, —, *Britannic* 76
—, —, *Cameronia* 38
—, —, *Cape Horn* 13
—, —, *City of Benares* 1
—, —, *City of Derby* 7, 10
—, —, *City of Edinburgh* 113
—, —, *City of London* 7, 10-11
—, —, *Clan Cummings* 7
—, —, *Clan Morrison* 7
—, —, *Costa Rica* 6, 9-10
—, —, *Delane* 7
—, —, *Devonshire* 123
—, —, *Dunedin* 7
—, —, *Dunera* 123
—, —, *Durban Castle* 29
—, —, *Elisabethville* 7, 10
—, —, *Ellenga* 115
—, —, *Empire Song* 7
—, —, *Empire Star* 124-6
—, —, *Empire Trooper* 6, 8
—, —, *Empire Woodlark* 114
—, —, *Empress of Asia* 123-4
—, —, *Empress of Canada* 11, 30
—, —, *Ernebank* 6
—, —, *Essex* 7
—, —, *Felix Roussel* 123-4
—, —, *Georgic* 18
—, —, *Highland Brigade* 31
—, —, *Highland Princess* 22, 57
—, —, *Ile de France* 61
—, —, *Khandalla* 76
—, —, *Leopoldville* 6
—, —, *Llangibby Castle* 76
—, —, *Lossiebank* 13
—, —, *Mahseer* 6
—, —, *Menelaus* 7
—, —, *Moreton Bay* 138
—, —, *Narwik* 92
—, —, *Neuralia* 6
—, —, *Nieuw Amsterdam* 114
—, —, *Northern Prince* 7
—, —, *Northumberland* 10, 12
—, —, *Oorangi* 114
—, —, *Orbita* 7, 77, 134
—, —, *Orcades* 92-5, 125

—, —, *Orestes* 23
—, —, *Plancius* 123
—, —, *Rangitiki* 7
—, —, *Rawnsley* 13, 15
—, —, *Settler* 7
—, —, *Stentor* 7
—, —, *Stirling Castle* 76, 138
—, —, *Strathmore* 75
—, —, *Strathnaver* 53, 76-7
—, —, *Tamaroa* 7
—, —, *Ulster Prince* 15
—, —, *Varela* 115
—, —, *Warwick Castle* 13
Shurlock, Wing Commander H.M. 37, 39-40, 42-7, 53, 55, 64-5, 74, 79, 81-2, 85-6, 100, 113, 133
Sims, Group Captain F.H. 86-8
Sinclair, Sir Archibald 79, 83
Singapore (see also under 'Ports') 20, 38, 46, 53, 56, 59-60, 63, 77, 95-6, 123-5
Smuts, Jan Christian 26, 94, 99-103, 136

Snowling, Captain 124
South Africa:
—, Afrikaaners in 34, 69, 71, 98, 101
—, defence forces of 17-18, 33-4, 37, 66, 97, 102-3, 136
—, government of 25-7, 94, 97, 100
—, military law of 48-9, 52, 98, 100
—, Nazi sympathizers in 92, 99-103, 118
—, press in 91, 95
Stewart, Colonel H.A. 33, 48, 68
Suda Bay 13, 15-17

Talbot, Admiral A.G. 110-12
Townsend, Wing Commander Peter 131

Vaughan-Jones, Captain H. 132

War Office 41, 45-6, 48, 51, 82, 85
Wilson, A.N. 136
Wilson, Roger 97